Praise for *HOW TO CONCEIVE OF A GIRL*

'Witty, emotionally powerful, and very crisp'
LOUISE ADLER, ABC-RN, *ARTS TODAY*

'If you immerse yourself and let the fragments accumulate, you get a new perspective on the messy, lateral workings of the human heart and mind. It's exhilarating.'
JENNY PAUSACKER, *THE AGE*

'A collection of writing that defies easy definition, combining short story, essay, montage and reverie, sometimes on the same page. Spencer moves from dreamlike fantasy to acute analysis… Rewarding and engrossing reading.'
PHILLIPA HAWKER, *MARIE CLARE*

'…will appeal to anyone with an interest in ways of breaking out of sequential narrative. Her montage or collage assembly of incidents and reflections, rearrangements of time and place, attract me enormously… The playfulness of the methods she employs and the self-questioning throughout…reflect an intellectual toughness that deserves to be encouraged and promoted.'
MICHAEL SHARKEY, *THE WEEKEND AUSTRALIAN*

'This is something really special… written with an elegance and eloquence that is inspiring. Spencer writes in the grey area between essay and story and poem… Her best is quite funny and sad and erotic.'
CITY WEEKLY

'The reworking of a classic text, mixed with contemporary theory and other elements of a common culture, is characteristic of Spencer's style and its strengths… Spencer's relation to history is genealogical, concerned with the web of connections that form the present and its subjectivities, tracing the complex, post-60s shifts in Australian culture and society which have affected her girls.'
PETER HUTCHINGS, *THE SYDNEY MORNING HERALD*

'Go with the flow when reading this. One connection invariably leads to another and, despite jagged edges, the prose glides.'
NADINE CRESSWELL-MYATT, *The Herald-Sun*

'At times [Spencer's stories] made me laugh, they constantly made me reflect, once or twice they made me cry… a talented and inspiring writer.'
ENZA GANDOLFO, *Australian Women's Book Review*

'Spencer writes with great verve and manages to weave together the threads of a colourful tapestry… *How to Conceive of a Girl* is an empowering, witty and incisive comment on the seventies and eighties sexual-cultural scene.'
THUY ON, *Overland*

'A prismatic and often stunningly drawn exploration of what it is to be a woman. As relevant today as it was when it was first published in the mid-90s, if not more so. Highly recommended.'
KIM KELLY, *Goodreads*

'A writer of exceptional sensitivity, precision and courage.'
PETER BISHOP, FORMER DIRECTOR OF VARUNA WRITERS' CENTRE

'By revealing that there's nothing "natural" about being/becoming/conceiving of a girl, by bringing this into language, literature and therefore culture, Spencer makes it more possible to rethink/renegotiate the social contract… [There are] dangers involved in broadening gender definitions, in boundary crossing, in abseiling and hang-glidings from secure subject positions; that is, in bringing the unknown, the unarticulated, the disavowed into cultural consciousness. It's a serious business… and I'm always grateful and amazed, renewed in my attempts to continue doing this when I read work like *How to Conceive of a Girl*. You could say that it en/genders courage.'
KATHLEEN MARY FALLON, *Australian Book Review*

'Beth Spencer flings herself into textual free-fall in this strange, delightful book… the collection simply buzzes. More please.'
The Good Weekend

Praise for THINGS IN A GLASS BOX

'Beth Spencer… uses poetics to nudge fiction over an edge. Episodic, surreal, tender and tough, these poems traverse suburbs studded with the encoded artifacts or 'things' of family, popular culture, memory and desire… *Things in a Glass Box* is a complex, considered and fine first collection filled with mercurial imagery underlined by aptly-timed perky jokes.'
PAMELA BROWN, *OVERLAND*

'*Things in a Glass Box* is… full of life, and love, tolerance and understanding, although many poems expose human foibles and fetishes. She exercises a rather kind humour and shows through her speaker a singular strength of self… Beth Spencer's poems, though tightly written, are expansive, freely expressing what is often repressed, those silent most active thoughts contained within spilling out into her lines.'
LYNETTE KIRBY, *AUSTRALIAN BOOK REVIEW*

'The souvenirs of the everyday… are scrutinised through television screens, train windows, cameras and display cases. Apparent transparencies become splintered to create new optics: these "things" collected and contained, far from amortised, suddenly look back at the viewer. This is writing as surprising and familiar as the repressed when it erupts into life; as piercing as pleasure or pain.'
ANNA GIBBS

Vagabondage

Beth Spencer writes within and across a range of genres. Her first book of poetry *Things in a Glass Box* was published by Five Islands Press in 1994. An audio version — produced in collaboration with sound artist Stuart Ewings — was broadcast on ABC-RN's *Poetica* and released on a CD, *Body of Words,* with other ABC pieces in 2004. *How to Conceive of a Girl* (fiction) was published by Vintage/Random House in 1996 and was runner-up for the Steele Rudd Award. She is also the recipient of *The Age* Short Story Award, the inaugural Dinny O'Hearn Fellowship, and several fellowships from the Literature Board of the Australia Council. She was awarded a PhD in 2006, and a book of her previously published essays, memoir and cross-genre writing, *Telling Stories,* and a bi-lingual (English-Chinese) selection of her poems, *The Party of Life*, are both due for publication in 2015. She lives on the Central Coast, New South Wales and has a website and blog at www.bethspencer.com.

Vagabondage

Beth Spencer

UWA PUBLISHING

First published in 2014 by
UWA Publishing
Crawley, Western Australia 6009
www.uwap.uwa.edu.au

UWAP is an imprint of UWA Publishing
a division of The University of Western Australia

THE UNIVERSITY OF
WESTERN AUSTRALIA

This book is copyright. Apart from any fair dealing for the purpose of private study, research, criticism or review, as permitted under the *Copyright Act 1968*, no part may be reproduced by any process without written permission. Enquiries should be made to the publisher.

Copyright © Beth Spencer 2014

The moral right of the author has been asserted.

National Library of Australia
Cataloguing-in-Publication entry:

> Spencer, Beth, 1958– author.
> Vagabondage / Beth Spencer.
> ISBN: 9781742586342 (paperback)
> Australian poetry.
> A821.4

Typeset in Bembo by Lasertype
Printed by Lightning Source

This project has been assisted by the Australian Government through the Australia Council, its arts funding and advisory body.

But couldn't everyone's life become a work of art?
Why should the lamp or the house be an art object,
but not your life?
                                            — Michel Foucault

Language has created the word 'loneliness'
to express the pain of being alone.
And it has created the word 'solitude'
to express the glory of being alone.
                                            — Paul Tillich

      Vag-a-bond-age – *noun* –
        1. The state of being stateless.
        2. In servitude to nomadism.
        3. Bound for somewhere.

Contents

Prologue   1
   Dear world,   3

Circles   5
   Leaving this house   7
   Dreaming home   9
   Loving stuff   13
   De-possession   14
   My garden, my sand mandala   17
   Free-fall (trust)   18

On the Road   21
   The party of life   23
   Advance to Erina Fair   28
   Advice for van-dwelling   30
   Truck stop   32
   Dog Park, Lilyfield   33
   Foraging   35

Being / Not   39
   On giving myself permission to not be a writer   41
   Where's Desi?   42
   Although maybe   43
   What's under the bed?   45
   Free camping (wild things)   46

Memory   49
   Forgetting   51
   The road to recovery   59
   The Shipwreck Coast   61
   To the whales at Warrnambool   74
   Carnage   76
   Snap   80

Freedom Is   83
   On Being / Inessential   85
   Fickle   89
   Reasons to leave   91
   Intimacy   98
   Show and Tell   100
   Structure vs Blob   103
   Wild things 2 (a serenade)   107

Summer   111
   Losing it   113
   The last hurrah   119
   Bush Santas   121
   Heat/wave   122
   Rescue me   124
   The pain body   125
   Learning to sit   126
   Facilities   128
   Inter-state   131

Lost and Found   133
   Lost Woman Looks for Herself   135
   The *Littlest Hobo* travels *Adventure Island*   137
   Small world   138
   Waiting for rain   141
   Singing us home   144

Notes on the text and acknowledgements   147

Prologue

Dear world,

I've sold my house
my ten year sanctuary and refuge.

My garden
wrestled from weeds and clay
is in new hands.

I've bought a campervan
because it seems

I can't afford a flat, after all
(Melbourne property prices: *boom!*).

I am a whisper
of butterflies

but here I come
(please make room).

With love, xxbeth

PS I plan to leave no trace.

Circles

Leaving this house

Leaving
is like breaking something

not a single crash smash on the floor
but a long drawn out rugged
exhausting
tearing asunder

God is in the details
as I pick them apart

The fine bones
The hush

I remember that first time
    unbidden
I heard it,
as I was outside walking
with my cup of tea
    singing
'I love my house and garden'
(a frequent refrain)
and there it was

    and it loves you

And I felt the pulse of it all,
strong and steady.

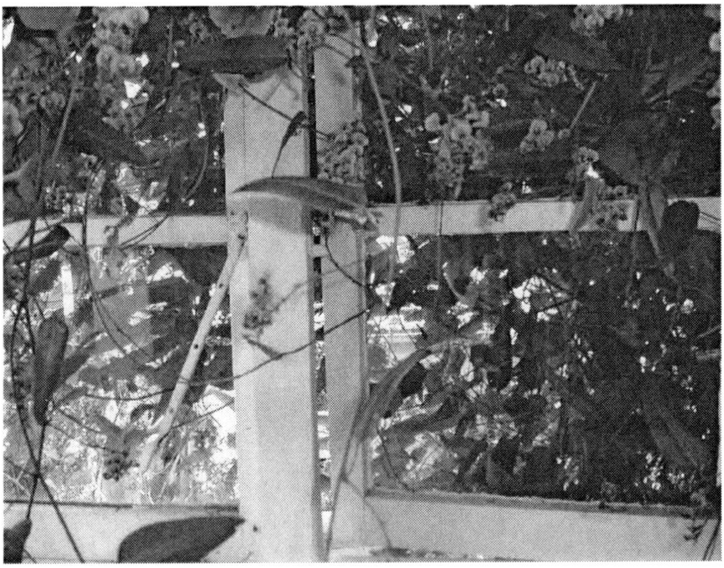

Dreaming home

On long Sunday drives to church
I learnt to read, sounding out the words on
real estate signs and billboards.

Up the Maroondah Highway,
over the bridge, past the paddocks,
past Dame Nellie Melba's house — that long high hedge and
(craning my neck) the caretaker's residence!
and maybe a glimpse through the gates —

braking slightly as we passed the road toll warning
(*Declare War on 1024!*)

— then zooming again and into the suburbs.

This imposing residence

Im-po-sing. Im-posing.

'What does imposing mean?'

Six in the car,
but no-one answers.

Maybe it was because
our house was already full before I arrived
that I fantasised so much
about a white cottage
and a front path
with violets up the sides
and a green door.

I'm not sure
if I recall furnishing it
with a husband and children…

Books, certainly. Lots.
And pens and a desk
and paper.

Sometimes,
my dreams went higher — more stories.
(Was that an attic window? —
Whoosh… too slow. Next time.)

And then on Christmas trips to the city
I would devour the opulence
of the gutted terraces on Victoria Parade.

Whelan the Wrecker Was Here!
(The magic man.)

Pastel walls, staircases, fireplaces,
ceiling roses,
another world, blasted open.
Quick! Feast your eyes.

'Oh, no, you wouldn't want to live in a terrace,'
my mother says. 'Dark horrible places.'

Like libraries. Like the one I discovered
in a tall old building down a side-street in Lilydale,
but was too frightened to enter.

(This *imposing* residence.)

But I did live in a terrace (several).

I brazenly entered many libraries.

I even got to hold
(although it took a few decades)
a book with my name on the cover.

And one day (another decade)
when I'd almost given up

I put the key in the door
of my first owned-home.

A miraculous cheapie
in a country town

with a green door
and a path curving from the gate.

And later, the thrill of discovering
under the weeds
— the violets.

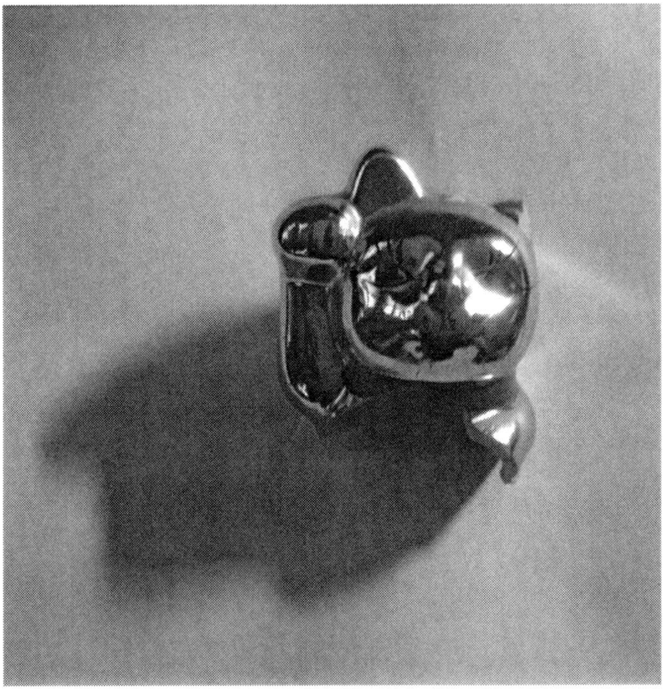

Loving stuff
(watching *Hoarders*)

    Have I become one of those
    people who
    used to have people
    but now have stuff?

    Things
    are safer
    (people,
    so complicated).

    Things are loveable,
    and *need* people
    (to look after them).

    Owning things means
    they belong
      right here.

    (Right here.)

    And they don't
    suddenly announce one day
    they are leaving.

De-possession
(hauling up the anchor)

I think, I say, I'll keep
my knick-knacks and artwork,
the special favourites I've collected.

The Persian men, for instance,
rescued from a neighbour
when I was fifteen (niece of the Shah,
made the most amazing rice)
just as she was ready to turf them out.
The ones everyone thought
repulsive
and strange
for years and now love.

And my found objects,
repurposed and rejigged.

And the paintings

— that one there
swapped for two batches
of home-made muesli
and a banana cake

— that haunting
one, unsigned,
bought for five dollars
at the Trash 'n Treasure

— those ones acquired
bargain-priced from friends
at early exhibitions

— and my collages
(made-it-myselfs).

They've been
with me so long, I say,
they are part of me.

Integral to my story.

They define me, really.

Yes, says my friend, *and*

all the more reason
to let them go.

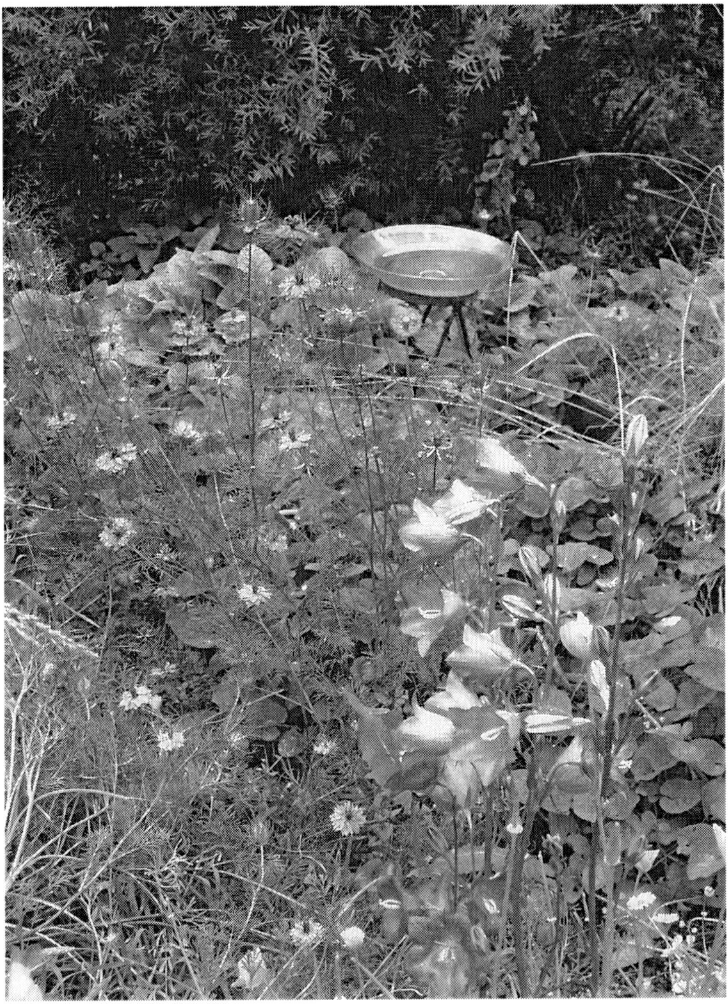

My garden, my sand mandala

In the town hall the visiting monks
trickle coloured sand
for days
in delicate, intricate patterns

And when it is perfect, spectacular,
they take out their soft fine brooms
and sweep it up

Free-fall (trust)

In between packing cleaning sorting
and scouring the web for a van

I become obsessed
with videos
of people jumping out of planes

Two favourites:

1) a woman
screaming non-stop in the plane

Blood-curdling screams
as she is methodically connected up
to her instructor-buddy
Manic screams as her buddy frog-marches her
to the open door
Blue murder as he
firmly and persistently prises her fingers off the door frame
Like a banshee
as he shoves them both
    out into nothingness

no foothold   no grasp

then the air catching   holding her

the world   just an idea   (just a thought)

Laughing
as her feet touch the ground
and the parachute rolls like a magnificent wave behind her,
saying 'oh, do it again!'

    And

2)
The ninety year old
whose false teeth

              fly out
and are whooshed   away

when she opens her mouth
in delight

On the Road

'The foot feels the foot when it feels the ground'

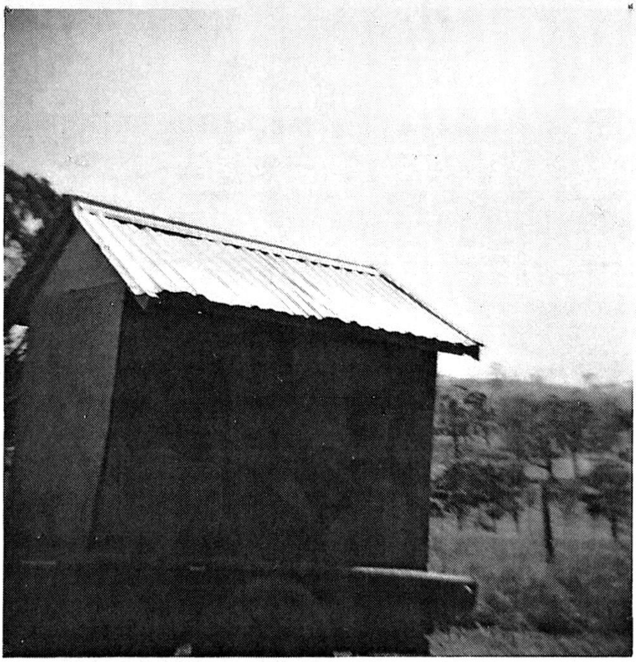

The party of life

For my twenty-fifth birthday
the invitation said 'wear black.'

An old primary school photo
with my anxious face circled
(including the big white bow in my hair)
had an arrow and the words
'Will this girl make it to 25?'
scrawled across the bottom.

Perhaps it was those sixties cartoons
that declared 'Never trust anyone over…'

Or maybe I just always knew
I would burn myself out by then.

Each new crack in my heart —
each new cut of experience —
digging a grave in soft soil.

So we called it an 'instead-of-a-suicide party'
and told them to wear black.

In the kitchen my housemates
prepared a storyboard
out of the pickings from
a cardboard box of photos and souvenirs.

Below a snap of my cubby house up on a trailer
(taken on the day it was given away to neighbours)
Lynne wrote: 'Never knew a permanent home'
and stuck a pin in it.

Ridiculously, we fought over this.
The historian,
versus the journalists and fabulists.

I was over-ruled, of course
(howled down / wriggling).
They evicted me from the party room
(after all, I was dead).
Leaving them free to sift and
interpret the traces
with latitude and glee.
(Never let the facts, etc.)

    And here I think about this
    twenty-five years older and wiser,
    as I draw the curtains inside my
    hightop campervan,
    wash my cup and plate,
    climb into my narrow bed…

On the evening of my twenty-fifth birthday
I was shoo-ed out of the kitchen
away from the party food
and commanded to lie in state in my bedroom.

So I put on my Miss Havisham wedding dress
(complete with faint patches of mildew)
and arranged myself on top of the covers.

Jill's boyfriend came to keep me company,
sitting quietly in his black turtleneck,
my unofficial confessor.

Each time I heard the girls calling
'Oh she makes a lovely corpse'
— their voices drifting down the hallway —

I stubbed out my cigarette,
stashed the champagne under the bed,
clasped my rose, closed my eyes,
crossed my bare feet neatly.

Mostly, the guests were speechless.
The flickering candles,
the baby-powder on my face.
The bandaids just visible at the edges of my wrists.

(Did we go overboard?)

Even the trendy-punks from down the street
muttered 'This is macabre'
and left.

Only Theresa and Jenny
after pausing in the doorway for
just a heartbeat (or two, maybe three)
flung themselves at my feet weeping, wailing
and gnashing their teeth.

As they recounted our lives together
('Oh, remember when, remember when…')
I smiled a secret smile in the candlelit dark.

Outside, in the bright living room
the guests bonded over
the polystyrene tombstone,
the epitaph from Plath,
the black crepe-paper-chains
and the cardboard coffin
containing the dips and chips.

The volume grew steadily
as they became ever more exuberant
(relieved just to be alive).

Through the wall: voices rising, laughter, music.
— The Clash, Blondie,
Human League, Marvin Gaye —
every now and then
the brittle sound of a glass being smashed.

Never knew a permanent home.

I honestly can't say why that one rankled so much.

A fibro cubby house
with its fake Fred Flintstone-walls.
As if that was my childhood home —
that small, *that* flimsy?

('From the town of Bed-rock
there are things right out of
his-tory.')

But I guess it is true
I have always had
an urge (or a habit, not entirely conscious)
— a penchant —
to cast myself adrift,
trusting to the invisible parachute.

The schools I chose,
the uni where I knew no-one,
moving state,
jettisoning relationships.

Always an eye out for the clean slate,
the chance to reinvent
(write the storyboard).

At midnight on my twenty-fifth birthday
I rose
and joined the party in the living room.

We sang Happy Birthday and
Hip hip hooray.

And I shed the lace wedding dress
emerging whole in a vintage white mini
with a beaded neckline
and danced till dawn.
Virginal amid the inner city black.

I rise… I rise…

And now.
 Here I am
at fifty

(rising, rising)

trailing wisps of stuff down the highway
(the odd patch of mildew).

In a cubby house again on wheels,

still looking
for the living room.

Advance to Erina Fair

I love a sunburnt country
But when it gets too hot
It's really very very nice to
Advance to Erina Fair.

I love those far horizons
I love those jewelled seas
But give me air conditioning
Phew! And clean facilities.

Van-dwellers all
let us rejoice
for clean fac-il-ities!

(Amen.)
(Toot-toot!)

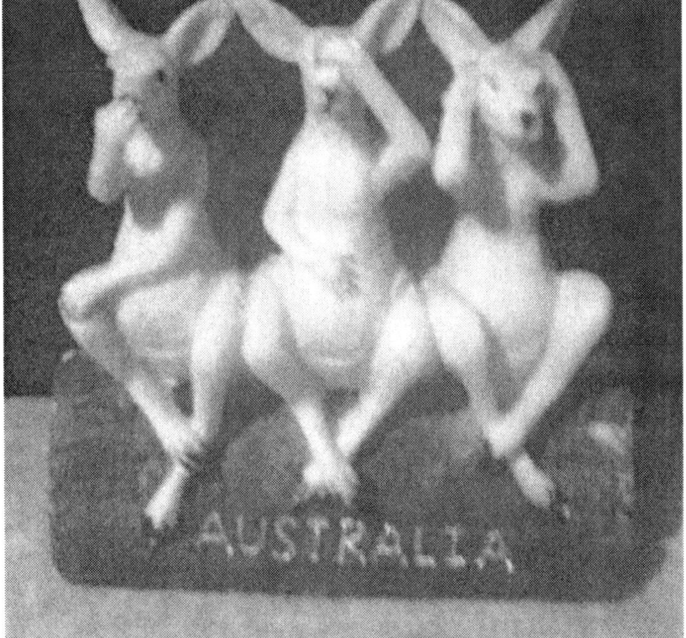
AUSTRALIA

Advice for van-dwelling
(after the US sub-prime mortgage crisis)

Don't tell anyone, especially co-workers.
Kitty litter, buckets and plastic shopping bags
make a good emergency toilet
Join a gym for the showers
Get a magnetic sign for the side
saying something like
'Plumbing' with a phone number attached
so you can park in side streets
and not look suspicious
No-through roads are good
Park right under street lights to deter car thieves
and mask light coming from inside your van
Never park in the same spot twice in a row
Have a pre-bedtime spot and only go
to your overnight spot
when you're ready to crash
Get good block-out curtains
Know how to protect yourself
(sleep with a knife
or a good strong piece of dowel
and know how to use it)
Buy lots of books
(Ok, I added that one myself)
Have good storage for food
Always dispose of leftovers or anything
that's had food in it as soon as possible
Have lots of good drinking water
Be aware of your surroundings and people nearby
Trust your instincts.

Instructions for use of L.P. Gas

Truck stop

I love a small house
that wraps
snug and warm, light rain on the roof,
kettle singing, fridge humming,
glow of the laptop,
bolster for a desk,
hot water-bottle nestling,
towel drying, sandy shoes,
ripe fruit
and a plate

and melting
through high windows
the clean soft
   edge
of a new night

Dog Park, Lilyfield
(9am Sunday)

Fairy the Rescued
  bounding joyfully
      diving
  headfirst into butts
       disturbing
the obedient
  stealing sips of
puppuccino
  smiling teeth tongue
tail flying
  basking
   in the *glory* of being
alive and beloved
  green sky birds water!
     home! and hosed!
        yes! yes!

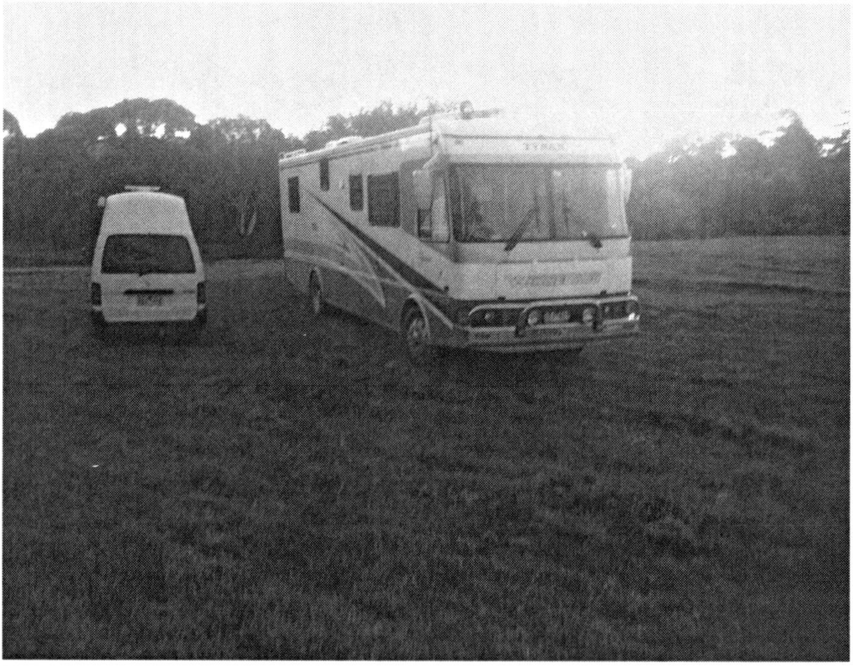

Foraging

On the path up ahead
a boy wanders
with his father.

A spring in the little boy's step
and suddenly he veers onto the grass
for an exuberant handstand.

'What are you doing? Get out of it!'
yells the father
'Dogs could have peed there!'

      *

At the check-out
a woman unloads her trolley:
everything plastic-wrapped,
pesticide-protected,
chemically treated.

Clean and safe.

No devilish insects had sex on her lettuce.
No animal urine touched her can of tomatoes.

      *

In my van I plug in my blender
and make a smoothie with banana,
water and fresh greens:

tender leaves of dandelion,
plantain, milk thistle, amaranth.

(Carefully washed.)

This is a good day,
so much to discover.

I savour the sweetness
under the stars.

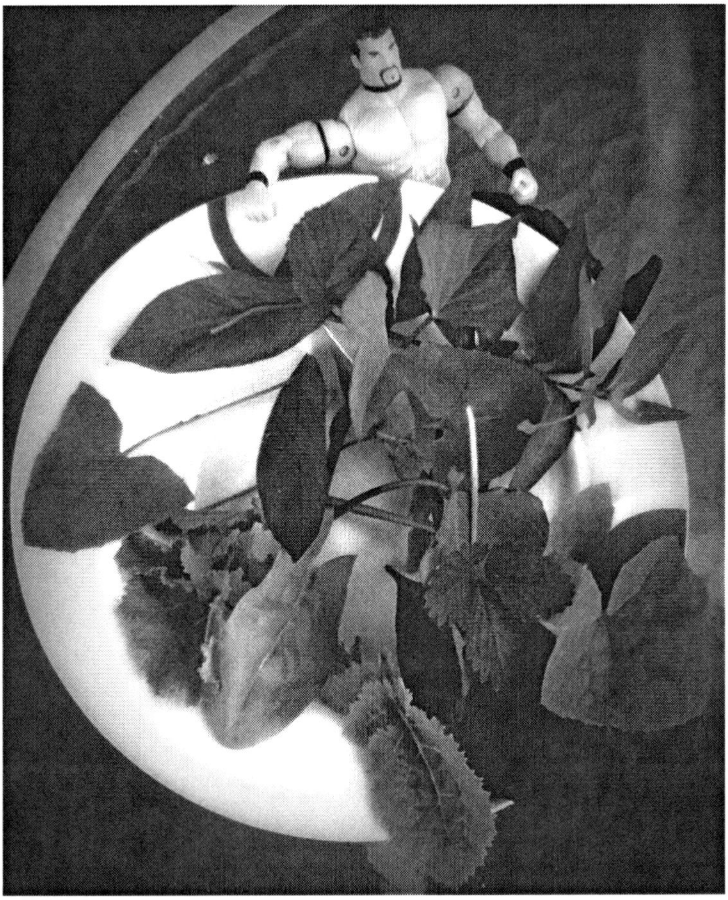

Being / Not

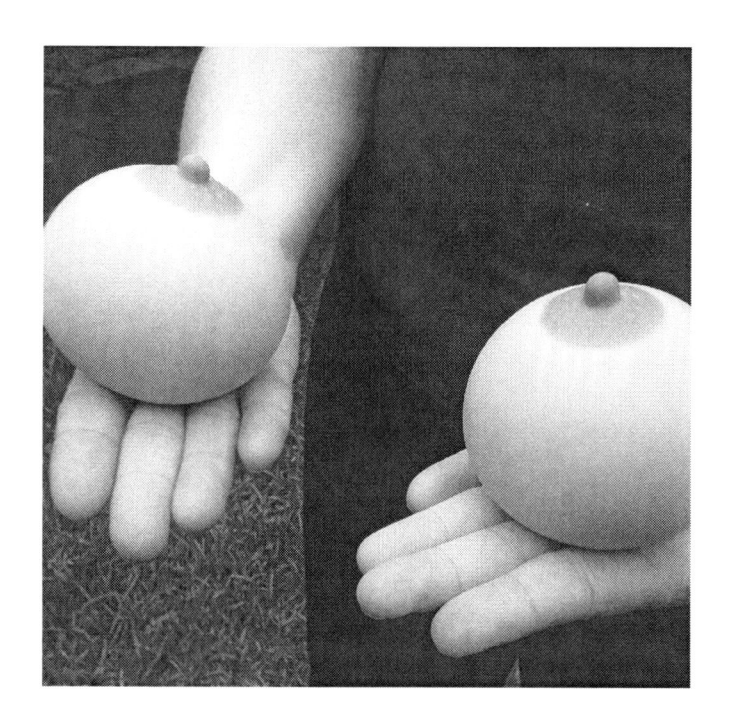

On giving myself permission to not be a writer (De-possession 2)

It took me eight months
To give myself permission

Not to be
That which had defined me
For so long

And when people asked
What do you do?
I would stutter and feel sick.

And then it felt calm.
For a while. Peaceful.

(The pain was gone.)

And then it felt strange
Like a terrible bit
Was missing.

(The joy? Can you have
joy without the pain?)

Nowdays
I am in rehab.

And I no longer say 'I am a writer.'
What I like to say is:

'Sometimes I write.'

Where's Desi?

Sometimes I like being alone
and sometimes I wonder
how did I get here —
how did I get so alone
so often
so many years in a row?

I imagine what it would be like
to have my Desi Arnaz at the wheel
while like Lucy in the back
I'm frying eggs
with my hair tied up
in a spotted scarf.

Although maybe

Or maybe I'd be
more like Mickey
with Goofy at the wheel
and I'm in the caravan
careening out over the edges
hanging out the back window
staring at the canyon
(that's a long drop, Mister)
only-just avoiding
being plastered
by the train (twice)
corn kernels flying
grabbing onto the *stop* sign
(in the nick of time)
then falling over and over
down the mountain
to land finally
click — connected.
On our merry way again.
Perfect.

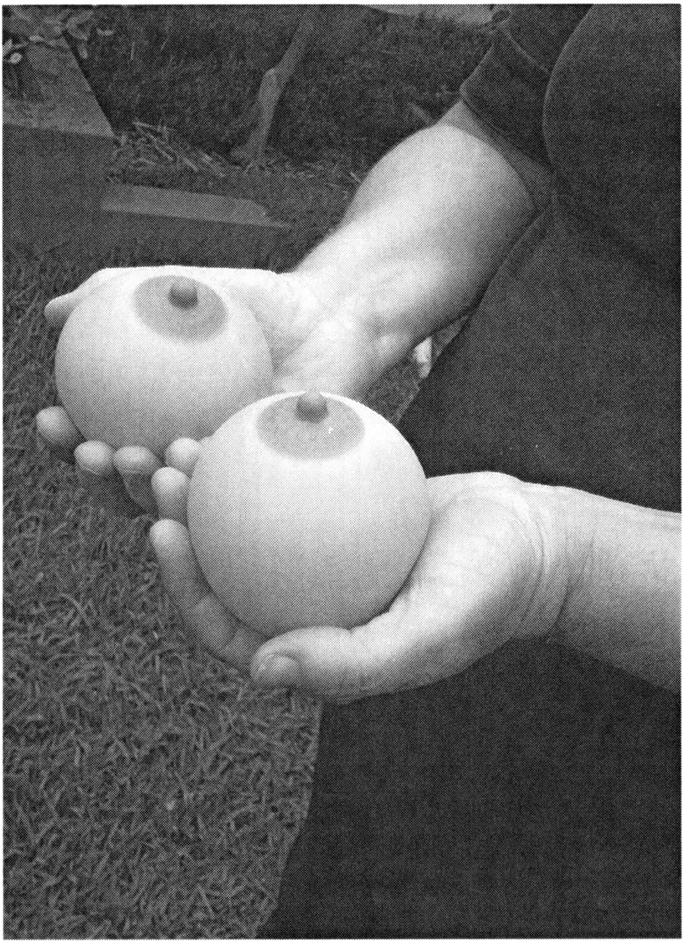

What's under the bed?
(*Bras and breasts poem*)

    I was sixteen when I found the perfect fit
    and seventeen when I threw it away

    Containing, restraining
    uplifting, constricting
    conferring protection
    and definition…

    Who needs it?

    Let 'em bounce

    And all these years later
    still perky

    Helen and I, having fun
    playing in her back garden
    taking snaps
       with two rubbery
       water-filled breasts
    from the two-dollar shop
    at the Cross

    And under the bed
    a box of notes
    a book I'll never write
    or maybe) (maybe
            I will.

Free camping (wild things)

I was thinking about the year
we planted the plastic flowers along the fence
(so hardy, no watering).

Was it the same year I ate the wattle seeds
to see if I might die?

Or the time I found that rusty knife?

I should have known the seeds were friendly
because the wattle sap was our chewing gum

— standing for hours beside the road,
picking off the choice bits —

always had a fascination with free food.

(Just for the taking!)

Wild things.

The rabbits my brothers would bring back from over the hill.
The blackberries in the gully.
The mushrooms I loved to collect in my billy
striding through the paddocks
eyes peeled for treasure.

Sadly, way too slimy and repulsive to stomach
though I was tempted each year
by the aroma.

(And of course by the *free food!*
free food! collected it myself aspect.
Pity about the slime.)

And here, beside a river, I eat kefir for breakfast
(nurtured it myself).

A culture of bacteria multiplying happily in milk,
an ecosystem in a jar.

(Loves to travel, thinking perhaps of those
years it spent riding on horseback over the Steppes.)

Thinking (me) about the billions of organisms
that make up 'me' (whole worlds)
and connect me out
into other worlds
through a skinful of critters.

A wilderness

of small things

(mattering).

And I too
am a wild thing

growing in my mother's womb,
unwanted
(wrong time, wrong place).

    Twisting and turning
    (can't get comfortable).

Entering the world

(in the witching hour)

   face up,
and
     howling.

Memory

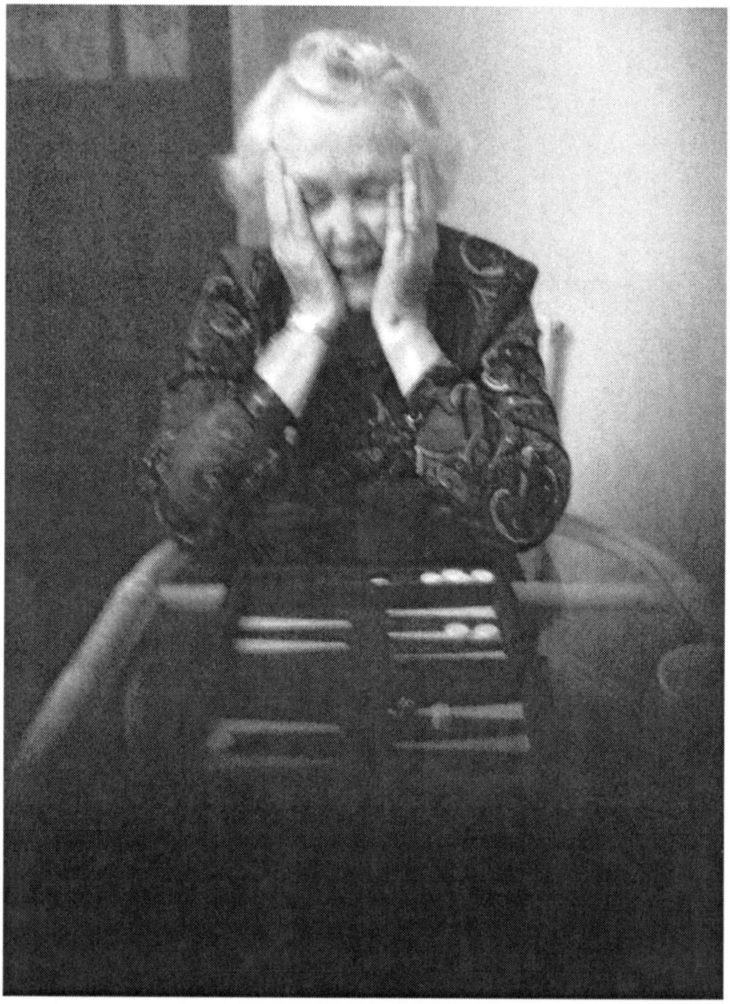

Forgetting

It was deep into winter
before I discovered
that outside the front of my ninety-year-old Mum's
Assisted Care Residence
was a great place to park and sleep.

In the old days this would be called a 'Home'.
Nowadays they've dropped the pretence.
A 'residence' or 'facility' is, after all, more accurate.

Because it's not your home, is it?

That's the thing you closed the door on
and gave back the key (forever) —
or your sons or daughters did for you.

Best not to mention it.

*

(Memories of my Grandmother
pleading at each visit —
'I want to go home. Take me home.'
And my mother steeling her heart
saying 'This is your Home, Ma,'
crying in the car afterwards.)

*

On my first night one of the staff
heading out at the end of her shift
catches me sliding open the door of the Van
holding my hot-water bottle and toothbrush.

She is fascinated. Delighted with the
the little cupboards and shelves,
stove and sink,
the inverter to charge my laptop and phone,
the skylight vent (installed by my brother),
the lush blue curtains, silky cushions,
brightly coloured mat and bedspread,
the gentle glow of the reading light.

I take her delight as permission.

A good quiet street
and facilities not far away
(in my Mum's private room).

Perfect, really.

By 9pm all the ladies and the gents
(mostly ladies, but some gents)
are tucked up in bed and the fog
of drug-assisted milky sleep
drifts out and envelopes my van on the curb.

I sleep like a baby.
Like a child in the back of the car
with a parent at the wheel.

      *

In the morning my Mum
glories in the chance to play hostess
— providing bathroom and toilet,
getting out her china cups,
filling them with hot water from the hall.

We breakfast at her little table.
In the afternoon I lie on her bed and she
carefully adjusts her tartan rug to cover my feet
and then stretches out in her recliner
and together we have a little nap.

Later we take a walk before dinner.
She plants her two hands firmly on her roller-walker.
Wearing her aviator sunglasses,
fawn trench-coat and burgundy hat and scarf,
she ploughs determinedly up the streets.

'Hey Lady,' a man concreting a driveway calls out.
'Careful you don't get booked for speeding!'

We play backgammon after dinner
— saving Rummy King
and Scrabble for another day.

I've heard my mother say she used to get
down on the floor and play games with her children.
If she did, I don't remember.

Or perhaps it was just with the older ones
before all the spaces in her life
filled up with children and work
and there was no room anymore
for frivolous things.

I teach her backgammon strategy, which is new to her,
and her competitive streak comes out.
It's a fight to the death. I cough and hint
when she is about to miss a chance and her fingers
hover, wiggling slightly, her brain processing

the cryptic information. Sometimes I subtly touch a piece
with the tip of a finger — and she lights up,
pouncing with glee. But the rest of the time I play hard.
No molly-coddling.

We become increasingly dramatic and noisy.
She beats me by one, and I groan
and sweep the pieces up like a bad sport
and we laugh.

We have a cup of tea and I sit there
quietly stunned that I had such fun with my Mum.

    *

Some days she is ok.
But other times, when she gets anxious
(watching the clock, for instance,
so she doesn't miss a mealtime)
her mind forgets to think in sequence
and goes around in a loop.

I've learnt that if I resist the loop
it can be enormously irritating.
But if I flow with the spirit of it
(see how many different ways I can
answer the same question, preferably with
increasing enthusiasm),
then time shudders and stops
and we start to float in an eternal now.

It is as if the universe
(inside my mother's head) regards
my replies as so fascinating
they are worth repeating again and again,

until I too start to see something
extraordinary in the texture of the sentences
and the intricate building of that bridge
between my experience and hers.

Gradually we weave a little deeper
into the heart of what we are saying,
until we start to perform something
beyond words. A dance.

   *

Sometimes I just tell her stories,
things I know of her childhood and mine.

She listens with a look of wonder and joy
as half-memories flit across and fly off.
Fascinating stories.
(The most fascinating story in the world.)

One day, after an hour of this,
she sits holding my hand
and looking out the window.

Then she turns to me and says
'So tell me, where did *we* meet?'

   *

On the day I hug my Mother goodbye,
knowing I'm heading north for some time,
I get a surge of feeling, a direct transfer of emotion,
a special mother-love-beam
that penetrates to my marrow.

I think: she is old.
I may never hug my mother again.

My sister and I have talked about how
the more she detaches from her old life
— the more she forgets and lives in the present,
the more the words strip away —
the more we are able to feel this pure
mother-love in a way that is quite new.

Or so old, perhaps,
from some pre-historic,
fluid time
(before symbols and words)
that we've forgotten.

      *

I think of closing the door of my house at Creswick
for the last time; wandering around the garden
one last time; and suddenly bursting into tears.

All the bittersweet in life.
All the departures into new worlds.

      *

She poses in front of the open side door of my Van
and I take a photo (a good photo – the kind she likes —
hair neatly combed, face full to the camera).
Then we reverse and she takes one of me.

She hugs me again, for a long time.
And then stands with her roller-walker at the gate,
refusing to go in until she has seen me leave.
She didn't sign out so I hope she doesn't wander off.

There is a fierce look of determination on her face
as I drive away.

And I can still feel
the imprint of her heart on mine.

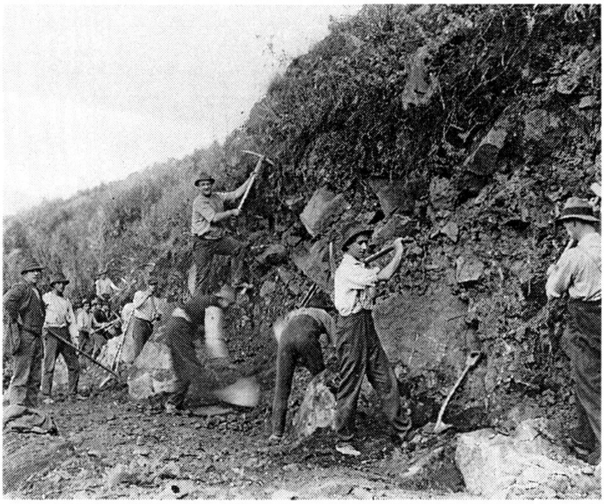

The road to recovery
(*a guide for tourists*)

> The Great Ocean Road is an engineering
> marvel, and the world's largest war memorial.
>
> Almost one hundred kilometres of the road
> hugs the ocean, often cut
> into sheer limestone and sandstone cliffs.
>
> Someone had the idea that working on the road
> would provide returned soldiers, having survived
> the Great War and the Spanish Flu,
> with a congenial place to
> 'think over proposals for their repatriation.'
>
> So they lived rough in camps, miles from towns,
> and in the years between 1919 and 1932,
> using picks, shovels, wheelbarrows and explosives,
> (carting detonators resting on their knees for the softest ride)
> they carved out a continuous stretch of road
> with spectacular views.
>
> Several lost their lives.
>
> There was no list kept
> of the men who made the road
> and their names are unknown.

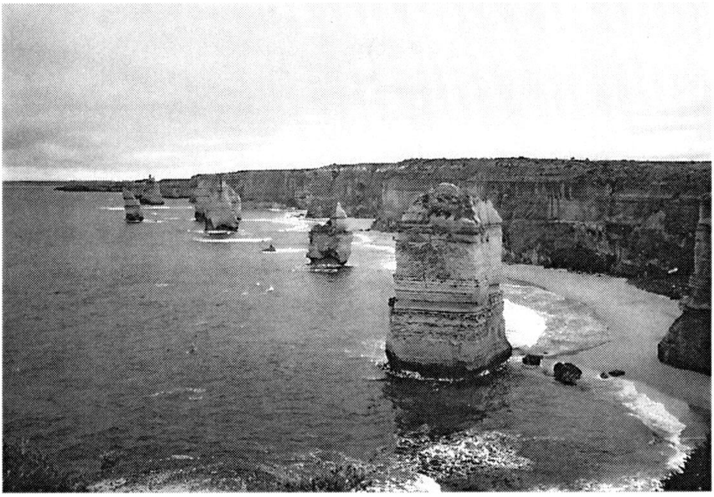

The Shipwreck Coast

'I have seldom seen
a more fearful section of coastline'
      — *Matthew Flinders*

Driving down the Great Ocean Road
(great ocean! great road!)
and my heart clenches.

It's twenty-one years since I drove here
in my white Toyota sedan (already a little rusty)
packed with books, files, clothes and a typewriter.

I had just been diagnosed with
chronic fatigue / post-viral blah blah whatever
and I needed rest I was told.

Fresh air seemed a good idea too.

Sydney — way too crazy busy.
And here was this house, vacant most of the winter,
cheap enough — and across the road — the ocean!

(A little sea-bathing to set me up forever.)

I had to learn to drive again
after a decade of buses, trains and walking.
A little skittery at first.

And I had to dismantle my life.

But hey, it was already crumbling.

While I'd just ended a long deep relationship,
my friends were busy nesting —
moving in with partners, buying houses,
consolidating careers, creating babies.

So goodbye job, goodbye share house,
farewell most of my possessions.

      *

(Now) at the end of a gravel road
in the national park
I stop my Van, make a cup of tea
and watch the remaining Apostles lovingly, savagely
being eroded by the waves.

Two millimetres a year, say the guide books,
with now and then a larger block calving
into the ocean, like the way London Bridge
fell apart in the middle.

Peterborough, the tiny town (one-shop-one-hotel)
where I stayed all those years ago
— at the start of my crazy shipwrecked
twenty-one years —
is next along.

      *

I feel an enormous
sadness

for that thirty year old
who thought 'rest'
meant going off alone, with a typewriter
and a few reams of paper.

(Feeling weak and vulnerable?
Try something harsh and challenging,
That'll do it.)

      *

Back then, within a month of arriving
I was diagnosed with more acronyms.

And so began even more
renunciation, relinquishing, peeling away.

No more wheat-rye-barley-oats-dairy-pork-
lamb-potatoes-tomatoes-lettuce-chillies-
spices-eggplants-capsicums-egg whites-
cucumber-citrus-bananas-tap-water…
And of course no alcohol or caffeine.

(I was so shocked and so hungry
when I got the results,
that I ate a meat pie!
Last meal of the condemned.)

But I was exhausted
and broken open,
willing to try anything.

I bought soy milk, rice flour and dried beans,
and made lots of soups and stews,
flavouring them with goats milk yoghurt
(which as one friend said, tasted a little
like a goat's armpit).

But look! The ocean!
Who could ever be unhappy with the ocean
just across the road? And books, and paper?

(It's going to be great! – the *great* ocean –
I'll finish my book,
I'll get well again…)

*

It was the tail end of winter when I arrived
and for weeks everything was
grey and beige.

Grey sky. Grey ocean. Greyish sand.
The grey-green rock stacks in the Bay of Martyrs.
And the vast constantly moving
grey of the wind-pruned scrub that stretched
inland and west as far as I could see.

The house — last on a street
of mostly holiday houses
vacant at this time of the year —
was disappointingly drab.

Hardi-plank. Not a stitch of plant-life
except for the wind-mown couch.

Beige carpet, beige walls,
olive-green laminex,
fake woodgrain cupboards.

There was a deck but it was too exposed
to the wind and the rain to ever sit out there.

*

I learnt to set a good fire.

My ritual (on a good day)
was to come in from my 'office'
(a bedroom off the deck)
just as the sun began to roll down and
wash the sky a darker grey.

I'd light the fire, turn on the television
(which only got one channel)
and watch *Degrassi Junior High*.

(I dreamt about the characters at night.)

      *

Outside, the plastic drink bottles full of water
that were strategically placed around a neighbour's yard
beguiled me into thinking that I'd landed in an
awful, empty but prim surburbia.

Until one morning I woke to find that dogs
had torn apart a rabbit on my front lawn.

My last residence had been Bondi.
Blue sky, blue-green ocean, yellow sand.
Life, food, colours, rich textures, rich smells and
sounds…

The grey beige relentlessness of my haven,
and the constant howling ripping of the wind
ate into my brain.

And then just as I was about to crack
one morning the sun came out.

And the wind relented just a little.

And I fell instantly in love.

       *

I wrote letters.
(No phone, and long before the
days of mobiles or email.)

If I could manage, I would sit for a while
at my makeshift desk
and look out over the crazy
wild horses in the ocean and the majestic Martyrs
— those rock islands rising squat and solid
out of the water, crowned with
wind-harried but tenacious green,
and circled by birds.

Every day that I could,
I walked on the beach.

I loved the drift-woody feel under my hand
of the staircase leading down from the
top of the cliffs.

Sometimes the bottom steps
were buried under sand dumped overnight
by the waves. Every day
a little different.

When the sun glinted on the cliffs,
revealing a jewel box of colours
and layers of lines and textures,
it was like walking amid prehistoric towers.

       *

I stopped wearing make-up and dying my hair
— for the chemicals, but also
because the birds and the wind didn't care.

I wore the same baggy clothes
day after day.

I became salty and weathered
and rarely bothered to look
into the tiny mirror in the laundry
unless it was shopping day in Warrnambool
or a rare trip to Melbourne to see friends.

    *

I became slightly reckless as a driver.
I loved the trip each week to do the shopping,
and even the journey to Melbourne, though it exhausted me
for days afterwards. But it filled me with joy
when I rounded the bend on the home stretch
and saw the sheep in the soft lumpy paddocks and beyond
them the ocean. I'd sing to myself and
yell out to the sheep and the waves, as loud as I could.

Until one day three little birds on the road
failed to get out of the way,
and I heard them — boop boop boop —
and saw them fly up a short way in the air
through my back window
and crash down onto the asphalt.
I slammed on the brakes, but it was done,
and I drove slower after that.

    *

— Being back meant
lighting the fire,

putting on a cup of green tea,
and *Degrassi*… (those sweet passionate young things,
so hard not to worry about them while I was away).

    *

At night, before bed, I put the fire out with the teapot
and I learnt to move the big armchair up against
the front door
so it wouldn't blow open.

Some nights I would lie under my borrowed
doonas and blankets with the wind screaming,
the windows rattling and the walls shaking.
And when I'd finally
fall asleep I'd wake suddenly from dreams of
waves crashing in through the glass doors
a few feet from my bed.

    *

I paddled through the days,
and then a letter would come —
a rejection or an opportunity lost —
and I would sink.

(Shattered.)

I'd rise eventually, of course.
Buoy myself up.
And then something else,
(something so small)
and I would come to grief again.

    *

Rising and sinking.
Is that a form of swimming?

    *

As the months passed and I didn't 'recover'
— and as the pages didn't fill up
(somehow my brain just didn't work like it used to)
a steady numbness set in. A deep shock.

    *

Meanwhile, the bouts of exhaustion were like
nothing I'd ever experienced.
Deep and bone-stripping.
Frightening in their intensity.

Some days it felt like my chest
had been carved out with a knife and there was
nothing, no life-force.

Most days my head felt like
a bucket of shit filled with razor blades.

Perhaps the worst was being so exhausted
and yet too wired to sleep.
Every nerve painfully alert.

    *

The feelings could be so total
it was hard to remember what it felt like
to not be overwhelmed by the slightest task.

Hard to believe that this mysterious thing
energy — that connects us

to ourselves, and to each other —
could ever be mine to command again.

And then bewilderingly it would pass.

And then it would come back again.

    *

Rising and sinking.

I've learnt to live better with it, although it
can still capture me so fully that it is
terrifying.

But struggling and panic only make it worse.

Patience. Let the waves
take you for a bit.

(But what to do with the
anger ,when you can barely *breathe*
let alone move
to get it out of your body?)

    *

Back then, on the days when I felt good
I loved the solitude
and the wildness.

As the weather warmed a little, I would look out my
window and see people walking on my beach.
(*My* beach! How dare they?)

I would gather driftwood
to add to the fire

and barely wonder where it came from,
how it turned up in my world.

Although once I found
a dead penguin on the beach,
its feathers slicked with oil.

Everything, after all, just a step away.

*

At the end of the five months
my tenancy was up, the house
wanted by holiday-makers,
and I had to make my way back to the city.

My car a little rustier.
My bank balance dipping
further into the red.

*

One afternoon in that last week, a blue wren came
and perched on the driver's side mirror
while I was backing out the car.

It chatted to me and to its reflection for ages.

And I cried when it left, because I wanted so badly to believe
it had a message for me.

*

I reach the Bay of Martyrs
just as the sun is setting
and pull the Van in amongst a forest of buses.

Across the road, the house, still there.

Beaten by the wind,
perhaps a little greyer,
strangely unchanged.

I watch it for a long time.
Then I turn and look out to the ocean
and consider following the wooden steps
down to the beach.

(My beach.

*All that beauty,
all that rage.*)

But the light is leaving quickly
and the sand is cold.

People are filing into their buses
and the doors clanging shut.

I close my eyes and listen to the waves,

then continue on.

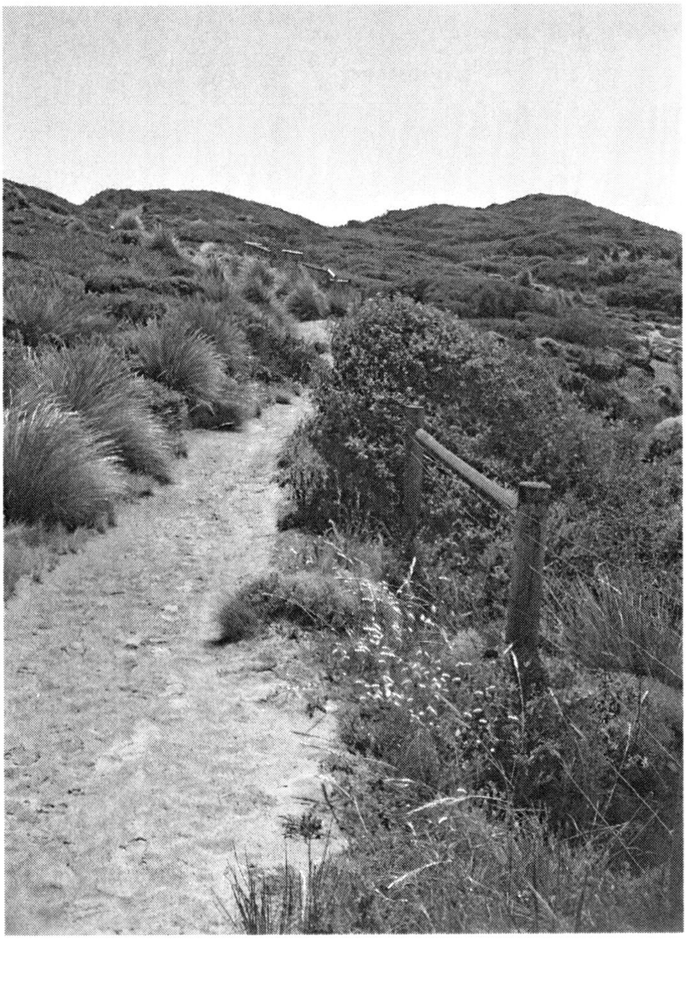

To the whales at Warrnambool
(*after Thomas Moore*)

    It is said
    about the dark night of the soul
    that when you're in the belly of the whale
    and all that you are experiencing
    is blackness and stillness
    and nobody knows where you are
    least of all yourself
    and it feels like every day there is
    no change
    and nothing

    that the thing to know
    is that the whale is always moving

    your job
    is simply this:

    to be ready
    when the time comes

    and the whale
    spits you out

    onto a new shore.

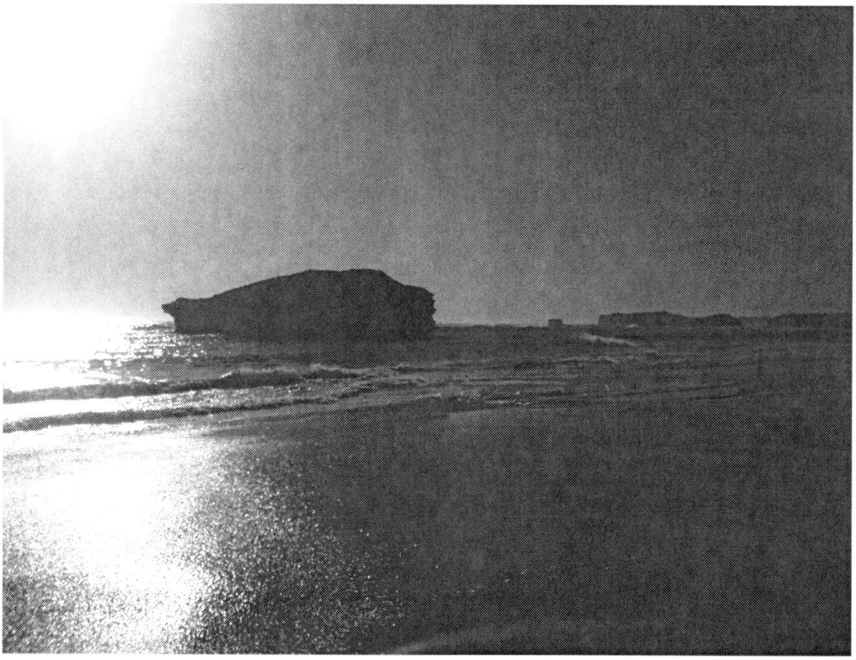

Carnage

I liked to tip my head back as a child
and watch the green tops of the trees against the sky
as we drove down Memorial Avenue.

So much beauty from grief.
Each small white rectangle
at the base of a tree holding a heart.

And then that strange morning
when the last tree sprouted flowers
and in white paint, the names of seven teenagers.

    *

So much road kill as I travel the highways.

Beside the white lines in the early morning light
still mounds of guts, blood and fur
that a few hours ago were warm.
(Possums, scurrying across territory to a favourite tree.
Swift-footed wallabies, determined wombats.)

As the sun comes up
the birds that come to peck at them
will be added to the toll.

And then a little further out at the edge of the bitumen
a punctuation of weathered crosses,
wreathes, plastic flowers, jars fallen askew and
tributes scattered and rustling in the wind.

    *

Progress, you see, demands sacrifice.

— Trees, for instance, are a danger.
Cut them back.

— Animals, a nuisance.
(See there in the headlights, and the soft thud.)

    *

On Anzac Day by accident I find myself
in the dim back section of a country museum.

Silently I wander among shelves of photos,
newspaper clippings and letters
telling parents their sons are not coming home.

Their eyes lock with mine
— all the sepia young men in slouch hats.

(A world in each. A *river* of tears.)

    *

— Be careful venturing out.
— Be careful trusting those ancient pathways.
— Be wary of that territorial desire.

    (An explosion of light /
        Bang!)

    *

In another part of the museum just one shelf,
unsorted and untagged. Utensils, spears,
boomerangs, sharpening-rocks, digging sticks.

And a still-intact dilly bag as if someone had just
laid it down and was coming back.

No names, or sepia eyes.

    *

The road spears
through the countryside.

'Countryside' — a word invented by roads.

As if *country*
had always been a side dish
and not the main.

    *

The countryside is so very dry this year, even in April.

And I remember sitting in the back seat
on long journeys through the Wimmera to visit relatives.
Staring out at wide yellow paddocks. I loved the flatness,
the vastness of sky. The straightness.
The movement of the car underneath.
The rare satisfaction of having both parents
in the front seat together.

Oblivious, as we drove through
unmarked graves, the ghosts of forests.

    *

How civilised we are, you see,

we no longer sacrifice virgins or cut the throats
of lambs on altars.

Lay down concrete and bitumen

and throw these, instead,
 under the wheels.

Snap
(*Saturday, 7 February 2009*)

    On an equine forum
    a conversation deals out
    like a hand of cards

        Where are the horses?
        Has anyone seen X?
        Where is the fire now?

    Then someone lays this down:

        All the houses
        on the north side of Steels Creek Road
        are gone

    Just like that (a puff of smoke / a magic trick)?

    Far away I lie safe
    on a wooden floor, face to a fan
    and close my eyes

    I see a blue bedroom
    on the west side of the house
    and wonder who slept there last night

    and did they still have the floral lino
    and the long shiny hallway
    and the separate boys' and girls' wardrobes?

    Did they have to climb out the window
    (as I discovered was possible one day
    when I was five)?

Or did they run through the house
past the 50s room divider in the kitchen
past the old wood stove
out through the gumboot-room
(with its purple and yellow paint
left-over from the dairy)?

Did they run down the back steps?

(Did they have a cat that always got
kicked down those steps
by booted feet when it tried to get inside,
or did one finally make it
into the living room to curl on the couch?)

I can hear the cows bellowing
Who is milking them tonight?

— Did someone remember to let the galah
and the cockatoo out of the cage made
from an old water tank and chicken-wire?

— Did someone let the dogs off the chains
near the post where
the hessian rubbish-bag hangs?

Under my eyelids I make a movie where all of them
get out early and
drive south down Steels Creek Road
with the trees burning above their heads,
like we did forty years ago

(Please don't let them stay inside,
please don't let them seek shelter
in the pink bathroom)

— Not so far, you see, the safe end of the road,
only five minutes and they'd be in the
town and could sit silently, shocked and spent,
out at the oval by the river

(Did someone hold a baby on their lap,
who will always always
have an aversion
to the colour orange?)

I curl my arms out to make a space
to hold that family safe

while our house on the hill goes up.

Freedom Is

On Being / Inessential

To be enjoyed,
but not   essential

no important cog in
anyone's machine

is liberating,
if you can handle the vertigo.

       *

Low on the priority list,
out of necessity

(partner, children,
aged parents, siblings,
work colleagues,
choir buddies,
children's-friends'-parents,
soccer coach,
therapist,
oh yes, and my beloved single friend).

Able to disappear
(no-one really notices).

       *

And I am practiced at this:
sixth child.

Once I hid
for a whole afternoon
behind the glory box

(blue, with the Queen's
wedding pictures in the
secret lift-up top).

If I could just sit here quietly, forever...

A poor-girl's substitute for running away
but where was an eight-year-old to go?

My mother
called and called.

When she found me,
she gave me a look
— a new one.

Puzzled,
(and a tinge of annoyed).

Not new enough
to break my invisibility spell.

"Tea's *ready*," exasperated.

I followed, meek.

But I saved the spoon,
tunnelling,
into worlds beyond.

    *

And now...
travelling travelling travelling
keep those paws a-moving!

(How did I get here?)

"You are so lucky!"

No chains,
no collars,
no golden ring that binds.

No green soft mossy cushion for
your fall.

(Drifter)

       (a red balloon)

       (the queendom of free).

Just another word.

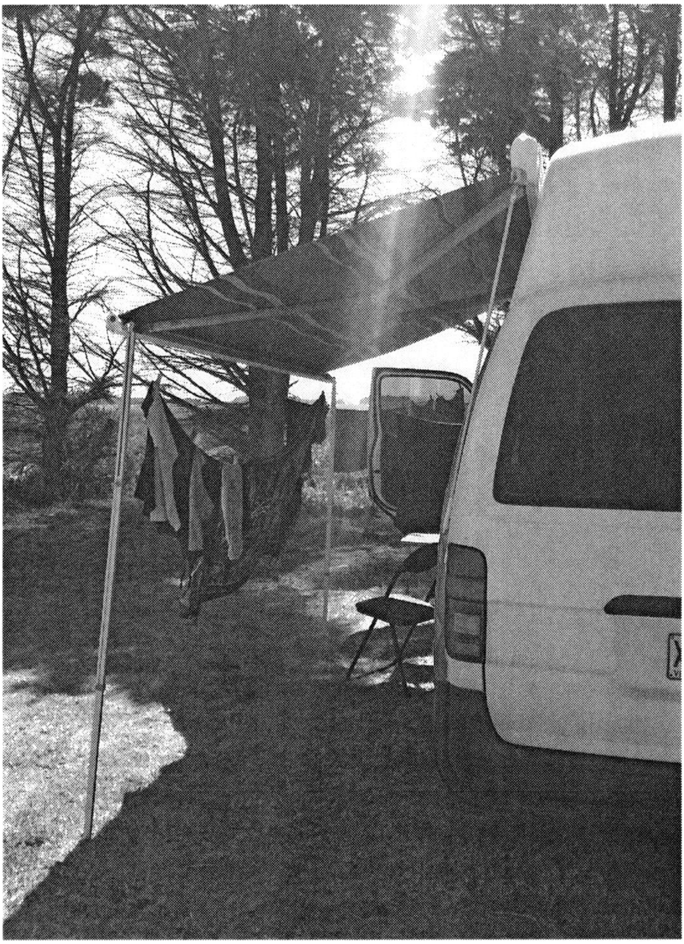

Fickle

At Anglesea Park my new friends
invite themselves to lunch
but don't bring a thing.
(Where's the manners in that?)

Their eyes follow each loaded fork
but when I offer carrot and salad,
after an initial flurry of excitement, they decline.

They peer shyly across the wooden picnic table
leaving me to carry the bulk of the conversation.

Then one gets up on the table top showing off
orange dancing shoes. Another ruffles a white pelisse.
A third creeps a little closer, confidingly,
on the seat beside me (enthralled by my story).

Until a car pulls up
and paper cups of hot chips emerge
(with a couple wrapped around them)

and suddenly I'm alone.

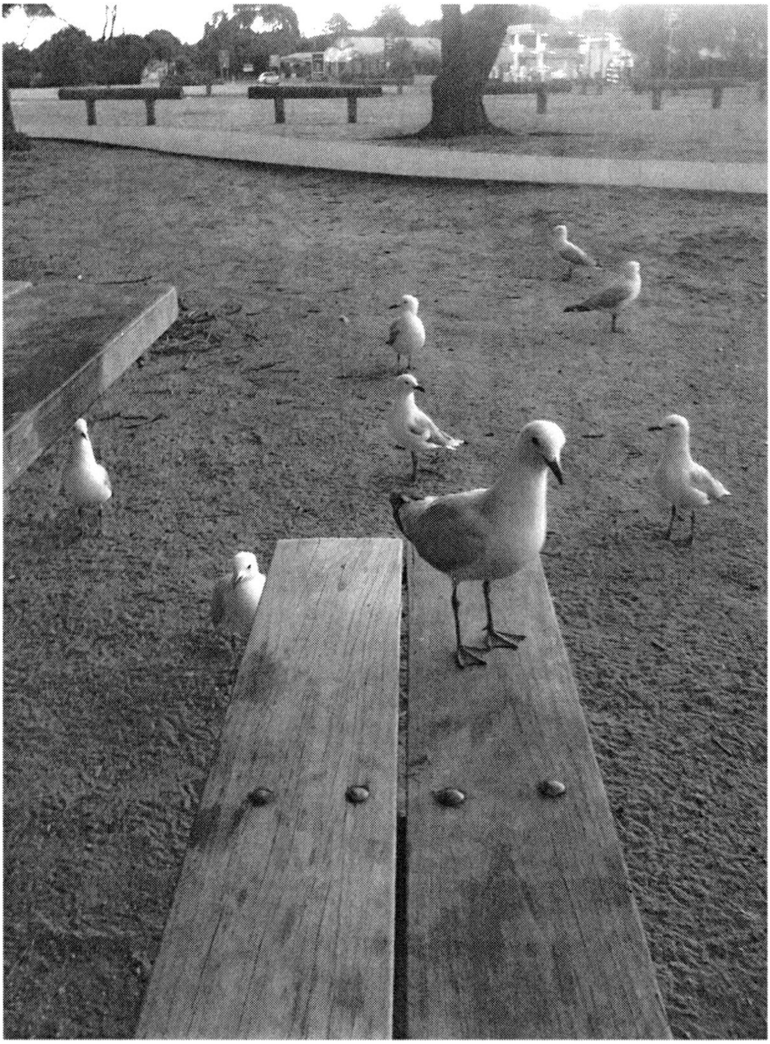

Reasons to leave

because my house battery in my van is going flat
the lights are flickering
and I need to go for a long drive to charge it up

because it's someone's birthday in another state
and I don't really have a good reason not to go
— although when I get there
I'll feel so strange and dislocated and odd
that I'll hover in the corner
and make another excuse and leave the next day

because you're having relatives over to stay
and I'll be in the way

because there's tension in the air
and I'm absorbing it like a sponge
and I've got to get out of here

because you just want to watch tv (really?)
and I've come all this way

because someone said something and
it made me feel uneasy
and I'm really tired and I can't process it well
so
I'm just going to drive an hour up the highway
and sleep at a truck stop instead

because I don't have anything to say
that's good
because I feel really lost and miserable
right now
so I'd rather not talk at all

because someone's invited me to lunch 200 ks away

because I have that itchy feet
gotta go feeling
(it's that *Littlest Hobo*
theme music starting up in my head again:
paws to the bitumen)

because, who knows? maybe there's
something better up the road

because no reason

because I don't want to outstay my welcome
(you have no idea how afraid I am of outstaying my welcome)

because I'm sensing tension
and I don't know why
(and I'm no help)

because I want more than this
and I don't know what it is

because there's gotta be more than this

because there's the whole of Australia out there!
and I'm not seeing it

because I'm in the way

I want a desk, and I'm cluttering up
your dining room table
making a mess

because I've been here a few days already
and you must be getting sick of me

because you haven't offered me a key
and I have to wait in the morning till I hear you get up
so I can come in and use the bathroom

because I've gotta go visit someone
because they're not well

because there's a workshop I've got to go to
and it's in another state

because I've just got to get out of here
and I don't know

I don't know, I don't know why

because I don't belong anywhere right now

because even though you said
make yourself at home,
this is not my home, this is your home
(and such a lovely one too)

because even though you said stay as long as you like
I'm not sure if your husband/wife is keen about that

because even though you're trying to make me welcome
and I really appreciate that
I just want to go somewhere and cry
and I need to be alone to do that

because I'll feel better once I've had a little trip
(pedal to the metal)
and then I'll come back and I'll be better, better company
(I'll sing in tune again, for my supper)

because I've just got to sort a few things out

I just need to close the curtains and
be somewhere that no-one knows me
(big solid trucks whizzing by)

because you all look so happy here together
I feel so outside of all of this
because you all have your rhythms and way of doing things
(I don't even know how to load the dishwasher properly)

because you've got to get everyone off to school tomorrow
and you need your space

because... I can't explain it

because I'm lost and I'm looking for something
and I've got to keep looking

because you're all busy and got a life
(I'm in the way)

because I feel naked and exposed
there's nowhere for me to hide here

because I feel like the poor spinster aunt
the charity case

because your home is so beautiful and your
family is so great and your career is going so well
and I am...

I am so happy for you (truly)
but I've gotta get out of here

because you are jealous of my freedom
and I can't explain how trapped I feel

because i have infinite choice
and it is paralysing
and the only way to break the paralysis
is to start moving again
in any direction

because I'm in your driveway
and I know you would prefer to put your car in here

because even though you really want me to stay
I'm sensing that your kids are getting sick of me

even though you really want me to stay
I don't think your parents do

and if they can't say that
there's that undercurrent
and that smidgeon of passive aggression
and I don't have a shell right now

because I'm swimming in this slow strange soup
at the moment (sinking, rising and falling)
and I can't think clearly

and because driving somewhere is
at least doing something

because I can pretend for a few hours
that I have somewhere to go

because you
want to hear about my
adventures
and I have nothing

and I'm so self-obsessed at the moment
that I don't know how to turn the conversation
around to you

because I'm the only constant in my life at the moment
and I can't find me anymore
I can't find me in conversations
and I can't find me in your home

so I have to get out on the road again
and keep looking

because I can listen to music while I drive
and soothe myself

because being here in your family is
triggering things from my own childhood
that I haven't yet resolved

because because because
because I can

and that is a dangerous thing.

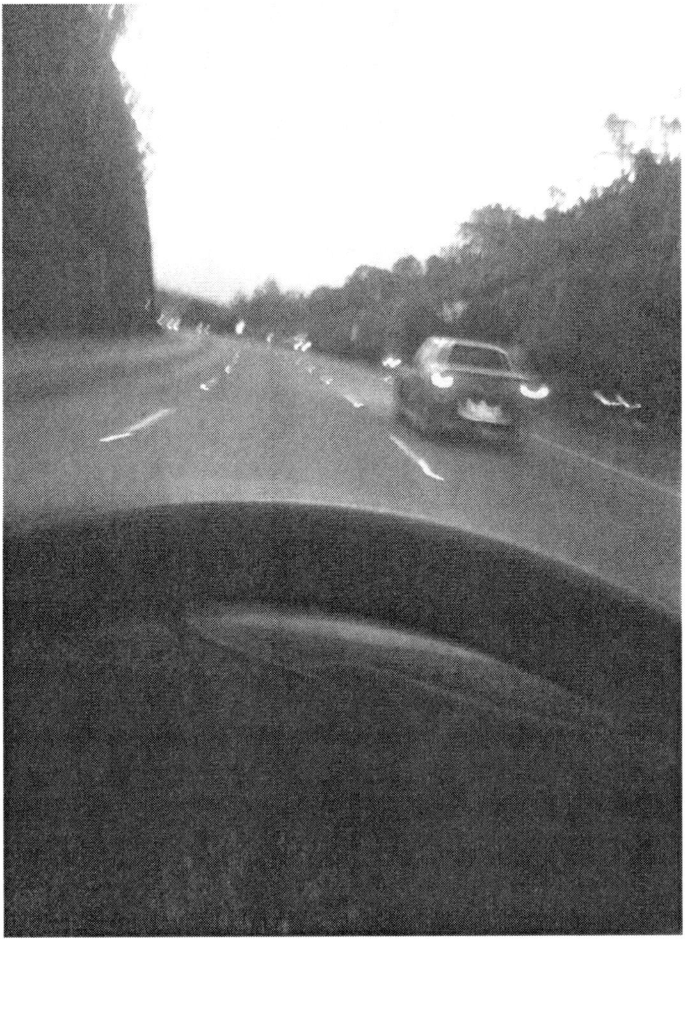

Intimacy

I like to go
away alone
to lick my wounds.

I wish I didn't.

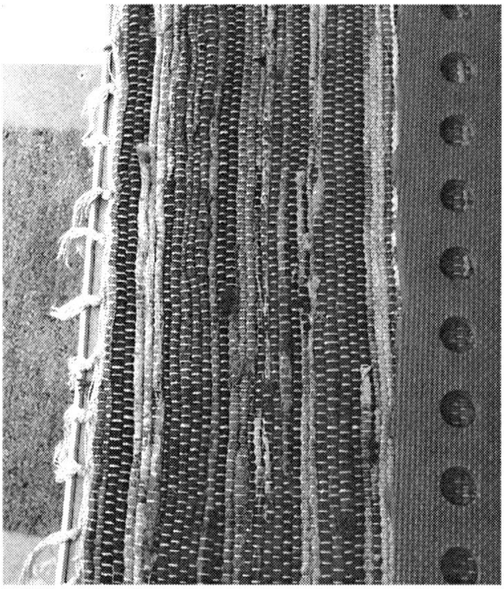

Show and Tell

I

At a book launch
I meet a poet I knew
a decade and a half ago.

In those years between
he's had
two marriages,
three children,
jobs, books, travel.

'What about you?' he says.
'Tell me everything!'

In the sudden beam
of his attention
I panic.

I am on the shelf.

Bookless, boneless.

My hands open
but empty.

II

Another time, giving a lift
to a man I've just met
and he draws me out as we head up the coast

until a picture emerges: all my many achievements
(many of which I'd considered failures).

In the warm
slow breath of his regard
I come alive.

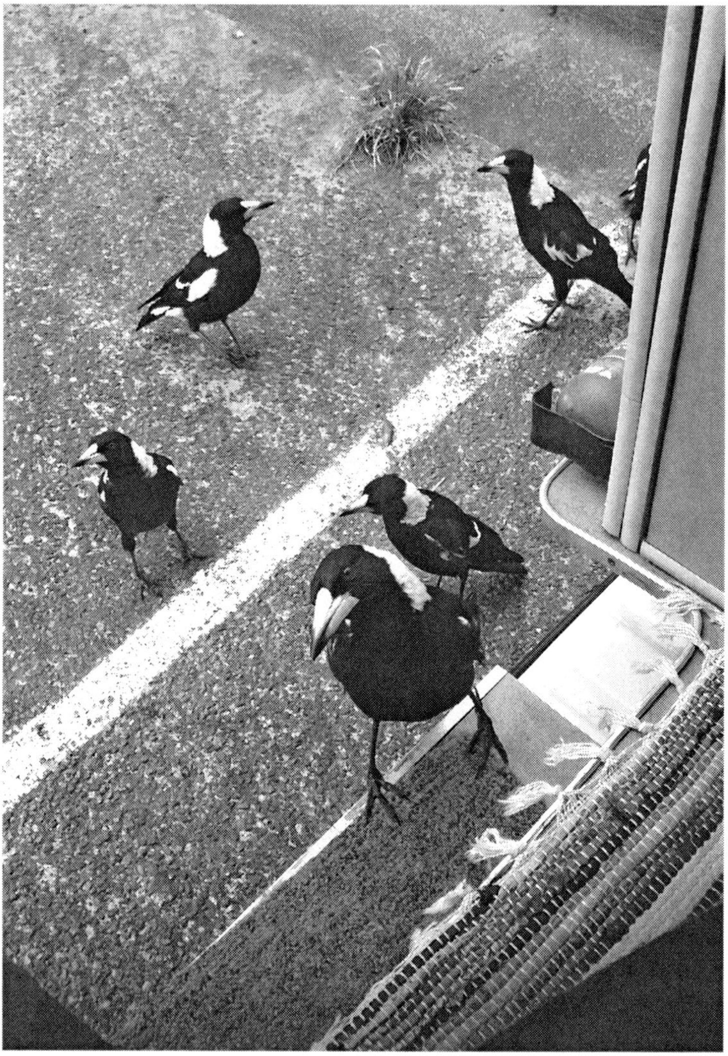

Structure vs Blob

It makes sense that we develop routines,
habits and boundaries

not to imprison
but to free

So that within the chosen
quarter acre
we can create
and produce

Protected from a thousand choices
every day,
endless decisions

(Where to sleep?
Where to go to the toilet?
Who to see next?)

A measured bargain between
the predictable and the
small and unexpected that enlivens

Indeed, nomads more than anyone
had laws and rituals

cultivating propinquity and familiarity to
breed contentment and peace

A fine balance

Certainty and uncertainty,
a delicate recipe

And now for a tincture of chaos
(but only a touch) —

Whoops! Too much!

Oh, *hold my breath…*

No, breathe, breathe,
Just breathe.

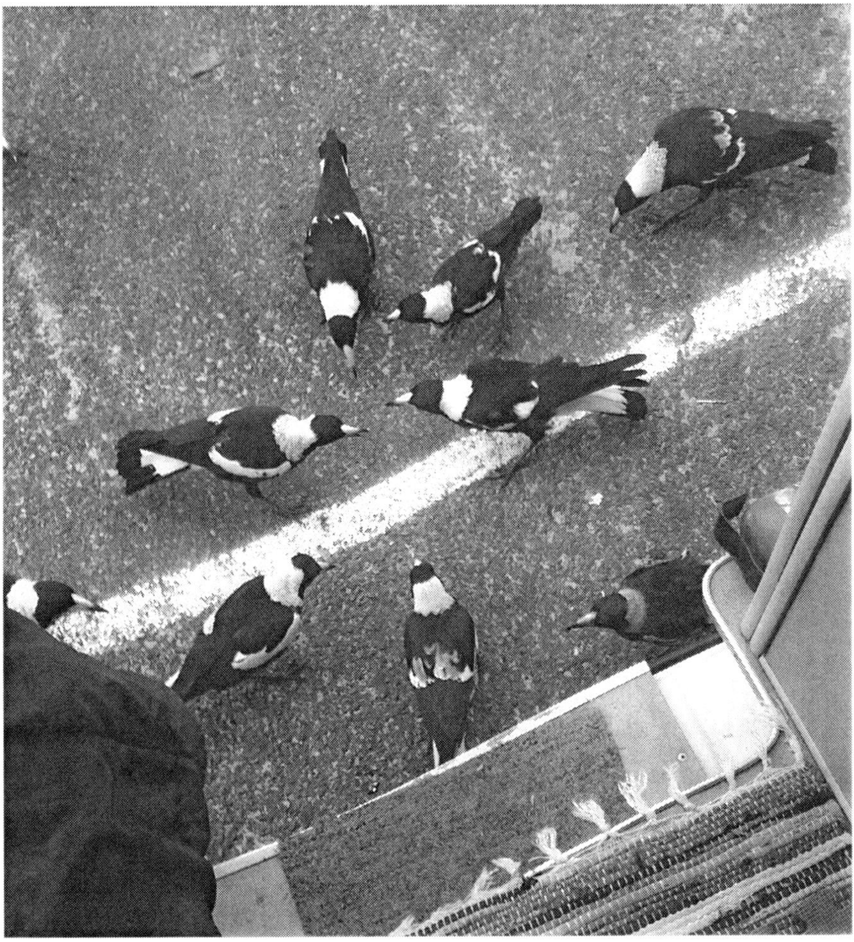

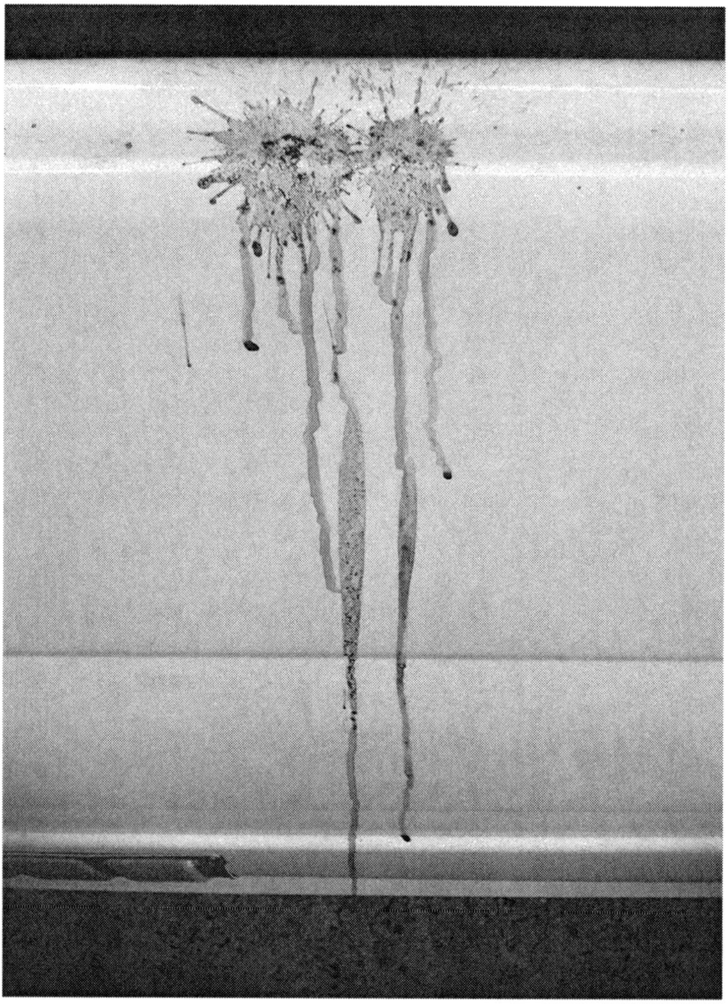

Wild things 2
(a serenade)

I would like to sing a song
to the loose, the wandering
and the unattached.

To those who cannot
grow themselves in rows
for the benefit of others.

I sing to the ones whose
invisible roots disappear down deep
into the earth to bring up treasure.

To those whose mutations
may one day prove beneficial
when all hope has failed.

To all those still unmet.

I salute the wild things!

— The untamed,
the disarrayed.

The ones impelled by their
own sweet strange DNA
to take hold
even when life is harsh
and keeps   slipping
out of reach.

Extending under fences
to the despair of gardeners.

Offering themselves
— as roughage
and shade.

Striding forth
in the wake of the bulldozer
— first after the fire
— bedding themselves
into clay and shaking it.

Opportunists, diagnosticians,
red flag wavers.

Signallers of deficiencies
and imbalance.

Resisters
to the end.

I salute
even those
that in the presence of
   crimes
    ignorance
    neglect
    greed
become thugs (*a mirror*).

The ones saying:
   'Too much here in too few hands!
   Too much and too long a disrespect
   (of the sensitive and their protectors,
   the rare and the different).
   Too indiscriminate, poisonous!
   And I will take it back

    and take it over
    and create a tide of seed that
    covers everything
    and entangles generations.'

I salute you
O wise and terrible weeds.

The tasty,
and the bitter.

The nourishing
and the deadly.

I honor that small wisp
that separates you
from fruit and flowers,

and the crack in me

that holds you dormant

    until ready or not.

Summer

Losing it

He of the sensuous deep voice
is my companion of the highway
and some days I love him to bits

when he faithfully steers me through a strange city
or along an unfamiliar road.

So patient. Right there at my side.

But…

Well, our relationship is not perfect.
(Under-statement.)

Tell me, why is it,
when most of the time he gives
an unnecessary amount of warnings

(Turn right in 200 metres…
turn right in 150 metres… turn right…)

other times it's as if he's been filing his nails,
then suddenly looks up and says
— Turn right in 10 metres!
and I have to veer madly across the lanes?

And what about that day
in the middle of the city during peak hour
when he kept changing his mind?

— Turn right at the next intersection.

So I perilously manoeuvre myself across three lanes,
only for him to abruptly say

— Turn left.

What?

— Turn left.
— Turn right.
— Turn left in 50 metres.
— Turn right!

Till I am screaming,
Make up your mind, you maniac!

But he is impervious.

And, after a haughty pause,
continues in the same know-it-all tone
— Turn left in 10 metres.

I can't. That's a parking station!

(I don't believe I've ever felt so angry in my life
as I've been with him.

Why is that?

Is it because normally he is so dependable,
and to then suddenly let me down like this
when I need him most?

Is this what it's like in a marriage?)

You — bastard!

(Sometimes I scream so much
my throat hurts.)

Where the fuck *am I?*

Worst of all is when,
after doing his little turn right–turn left caper for five minutes,
he suddenly shrugs and says

— GPS lost.
(in a bored voice)

I want to pick him up and hurl him out the window
so badly.

Especially
when I'm stuck in the middle of nowhere.

(And you brought me out here, you numbskull,
and I didn't bring a map because
you acted like you knew the way!)

In those times I can almost hear him saying,
— Not my fault you bought a cheapie on Ebay.

And well, that's true,
which I admit once I've calmed down.

Pulling over to the side of the road,
deep slow breaths…

So I don't throw him out the window.
I am too dependent.
He is, after all, quite handy most of the time.

(And ok, yes, he is *right* most of the time.)

Although I don't like it when he judges me.

— You're *speeding* (in a disgusted voice).

Only a little bit, and I forgot.
Hey I have an idea, why don't you try driving?
Oh, that's right, you can't, can you?

But he still says it.
And although I hate the *way* he says it,
I do put on the brakes.

(Ok. Thank you. Crackbrain.)

And then, of course,
on the other side of the anger —

the sheer gratitude.

Those times when we are
in effortless synch and glide through the night together.
Me at the wheel, he by my side
loyally pointing out the way.

(He knows just where I want to go, just where I need to be.)

And I especially love those
moments when he
sounds so pleased with himself
and excited for me:

— You have arrived at your destination!

And we both do an invisible happy dance
and I want to plant a big wet kiss on his
smug lips.

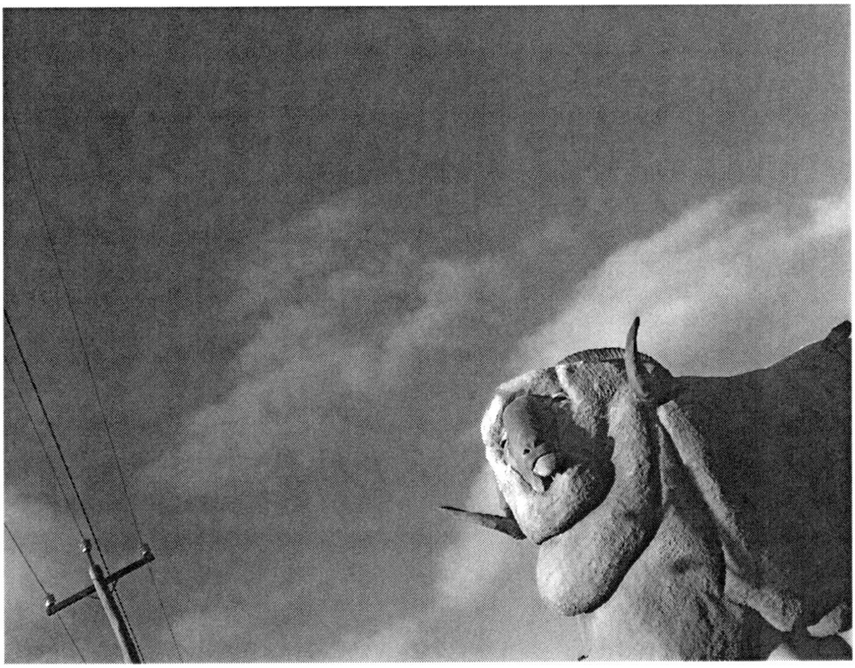

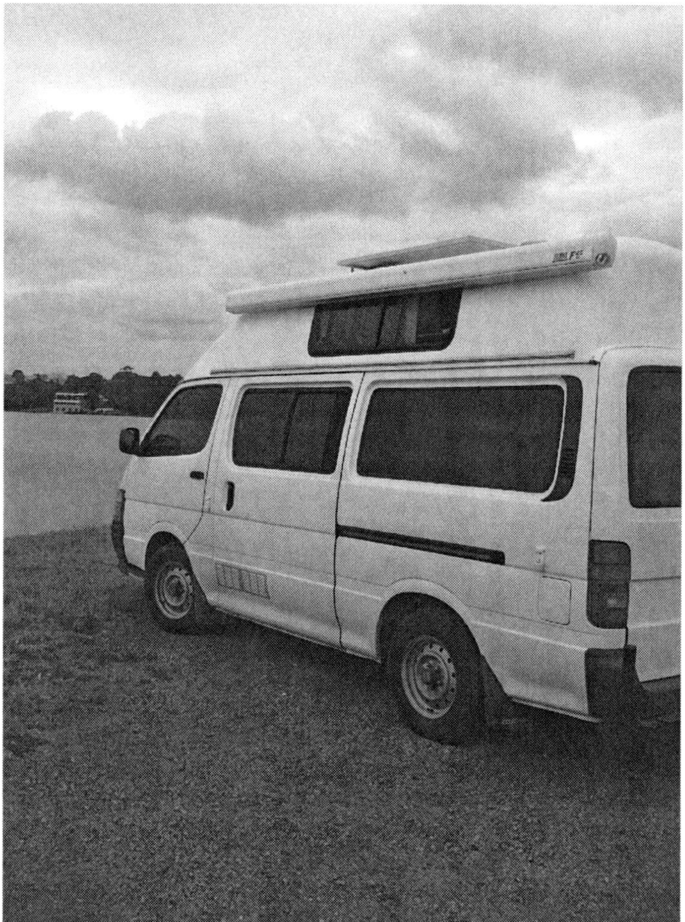

The last hurrah

In the park at Richmond River
the ibis converge on the scraps
like clumsy ballerinas.

One bites the tail of a water dragon
who stares at me
astonished, like perhaps
we knew each other
in a past life.

Across the way
a row of Queenslanders
lift their skirts
to avoid puddles and

cars drive by, headlights on,
even though it's 3pm (misty).

On the other side of the road
the Buck in black underpants
and bow tie sways groggily,
handcuffed to a no-standing sign.

His party bursts in a welter of
fancy costumes from the bottle shop
as a passing car toots its horn.

'Raaaayy!' they all cheer
and head back into the shop.

Another car passes,
'Raaaay' calls the lone Buck
miscalculating, the lost crowd.

At the grocery store
I buy some hooks and nails
in a small hardware section
with wooden floors
that smell of my childhood

— that place, a few weeks back
where I stood at the gate
to our old farm,
the ancient post firm
and resonant under my palm
but the house on the hill erased
by the Black Saturday fires.

Just a grey smudge now
against fresh green.

The Buck bows, when I pass by,
and I bow back.

In the park I sit and
watch the river,
tracing under my fingertips
the bouquets of hearts and
initials.

*(The wound of memory,
the fragile texture of cusps.)*

The water dragon returns
and eyes me slowly, thoughtfully,

then lifts its tail
and scurries away.

Bush Santas

I've caught him out several times, rounding a bend
miles from anywhere and there he is
in the middle of a paddock hopping a motor bike
speeding off with a full sack.

Or steering a team of corrugated kangaroos
using a cattle ramp as a launching pad.
Always in a hurry. (Big brown land.
So much to deliver. No pressure. Ha!)

And still wearing that   ridiculous
fur-trimmed red suit even on days
    hot enough
to melt the soles from your boots.

There he goes — straddling that post-and-rail fence.

I think of blowflies, 'santa snow' on the windows,
the smell of roast chicken and gravy. Plum puddings
with threepenny bits and a sweet milky custard.

And under the tree, my Christmas Dad
with his big farrier's hands
passing out presents.

Heat/wave

Mine was not a summer of love.

Too many days
revolving
around the search
for a shady tree.

And New Year's Eve —
sobbing
in a shopping mall,
so grateful for the aircon.

And that time I watched
Avatar 3D three times
so I could hide from a
38 degree day.

Outside
my Van,
like the road
laps up the heat,
trapping it

like a furnace

and at night
on my bed I lie
stifled,
dying for air
but too timid to open the windows.

And my skin burns at the slightest
kiss of the sun and

and I wilt like a plant
in each unfamiliar soil,
my fragile roots unestablished.

And yet…
I am living the dream
(well, someone's)

And I am embarrassed
to say
that all I want

All I want
All I want

is a house
a desk
running water

and the sigh (yes)
of an artificial breeze

and the kind of stillness
where it might
be possible one day
to compost myself

grow deep roots (yes)
and a bit of moss.

Rescue me

Then that guy
at the party said
'Do you need to be rescued?'

And I said, 'Yes, I do.'

And he looked at me for a moment
then furtively across to where
a woman was laughing in a group.

'Sorry,' he said.

'Not allowed.'

The pain body

    The ocean
    just ten metres away
    (a hop skip and jump)
    and yet here
    all the long afternoon
    I am
    locked locked
       wracked
     inside
    waves
      of my own
        making

Learning to sit
(the night of the 200 baby-tick bites)

At the Buddhist workshop
on anger
on the South Coast
I ask Rinpoche how he can sit
cross-legged for so many
hours at a time, and he says

Oh, I stopped having that conversation
with my legs
a long time ago.

That night I get bitten
by 200 baby ticks
and a conversation begins
with my legs that I cannot stop
no matter how I try.

It is a conversation that began
all those years ago when we drove down here
on that camping trip from hell.

What was it I said?
Something about the ice.

Then we were off. (Kapow!)

And I remember crying
while you threw my bags and boxes
out onto the dirt under a tree.

And I cried so much in the roadhouse
(my eyes and nose so red)
that the lady in the toilets was afraid I had SARS.

You came back, later,
and I packed my bags into your truck again
because frankly I had nowhere else to go.

And at night we argued and fucked
and argued again
and I felt almost free to see that
this is what people do.

This is how they say things to hurt.
But if you know that
you can let the knife slip over your skin
and not penetrate.

…Until that one time the tip
goes in
and breaks off.

So, you see, those little baby ticks
(I lost count at 100 on just one leg)
dug themselves in
to have this (necessary) conversation
squirted their poison
to remind me
(insistently)

that I do *not* like the South Coast
    I do not like

these memory places
of tears and pain.

Facilities

Ladies and Gents, I thank you

For the cleansing rituals and needs of the day
met in a hundred different spots
(thank you, kind citizenry).

All the towns with a special block for ablutions,
however humble (indeed I am).

Although may I say, I'm not so fond of those
unisex toilets at truck stops. (Please note,
some men really do seem to be
rather careless and aimless. Is it a territory
marking thing?)

But better these than none.

(Apologies for ingratitude. The trick seems to be
sturdy shoes, and lifting one's pant's legs up,
i.e. — hold them up at the knees so the bottoms
don't touch *anything*. Quite a feat. Takes practice.
Storm pegs might help.)

Also not so fond of the drop toilets
in a crowded rest stop in the mornings.
But — so ecological! How clever.
(Just make sure you get
in and out quick, and hold your nose, delicately.)

As for those space-age ones —
with buttons to enter and exit —
the ones that flush the walls
if you stay too long… Freaky. (But durable.)

Mostly, I like the ones open to the air at the top,
clean and simple, bluestone walls in
a long-remembered design. Locks intact.
Salty smelling from sand tracked in.

And what a marvel —
the great miracle of
running and flushing water,
carrying away all the dirt
and detritus of a previous day
without judgement.

I will never again take thee for granted!
O running water taps, and
my beloved Ladies and Gents.

And while I'm here may I also add
a little thank you
to the dedicated council soul
in Toowoon Bay who thought to place
a sign in each of the cubicles
saying
'Not safe for drinking'

just in case
you might be tempted.

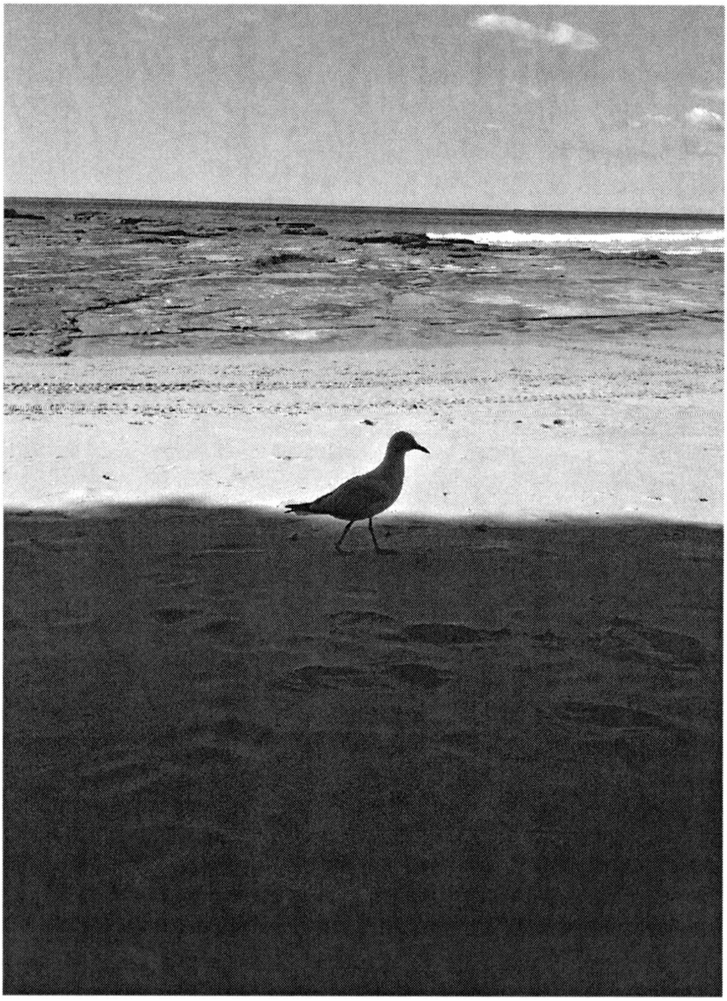

Inter-state

Driving in the dark
With Lucinda and Marvin,
Gillian and Curtis.

Glancing
in the rearview mirror.

Cruising.

Punctual. (Nowhere to be.)

Pondering

what someone
said:

— 'The partner
you chose, so far,
in this life,
    is yourself.'

Oh my darling.

(Not much left to lose.)

My sweet
    vagabondage.

Lost and Found

Lost Woman Looks for Herself
(*found poem*)

A foreign tourist is reported missing
in the volcanic canyon Eldgjá in the southern
highlands of Iceland on a Saturday afternoon
when she fails to return to her tour bus.

The driver waits
one hour before he notifies police.

Fifty people search
in vehicles, by foot.
Even a helicopter is prepared
but is delayed by fog.

And then at 3 in the morning
the search is called off.

The missing woman
has been on the bus all along.

The woman,
the Chief of Police in Hvolsvöllur said,
was innocent of the mistake.

She even participated
in the search for herself.

It seems that before she re-entered
the bus after the stop
she changed her clothes and freshened up,
and the other passengers
failed to recognise her.

She too failed to recognise
the description of herself.

She had, said the Chief of Police,
'no idea that she was missing.'

The *Littlest Hobo* travels *Adventure Island*

Well I followed the guiding star

but sometimes I think I might prefer my
car-ar-avan in one spot, with flowers out the front
and a little chimney
like Clown and Lisa and Mrs Flower Potts.

Maybe tomorrow.
(Keep those paws a-moving…)

Oh, dogs, such loyal comedians.
(Gauche, needy.)

Always digging up the bone
that everyone wished was still buried

and depositing it
with a grin
on the living room floor.

Small world

Outside, the footy players
shout to each other
and parents wrapped in scarves and coats
call encouragement.

Inside my van, I lean back into cushions
with my laptop and tissues.

My coach
half a planet away
talks into her computer
in a lamp-lit room

and I talk into mine.

We dig into the past
to bring me into the present.

Turning the soil,
Sifting out the rubbish,
planting seeds.

I travel the universe
(out to the stars)
and back again.

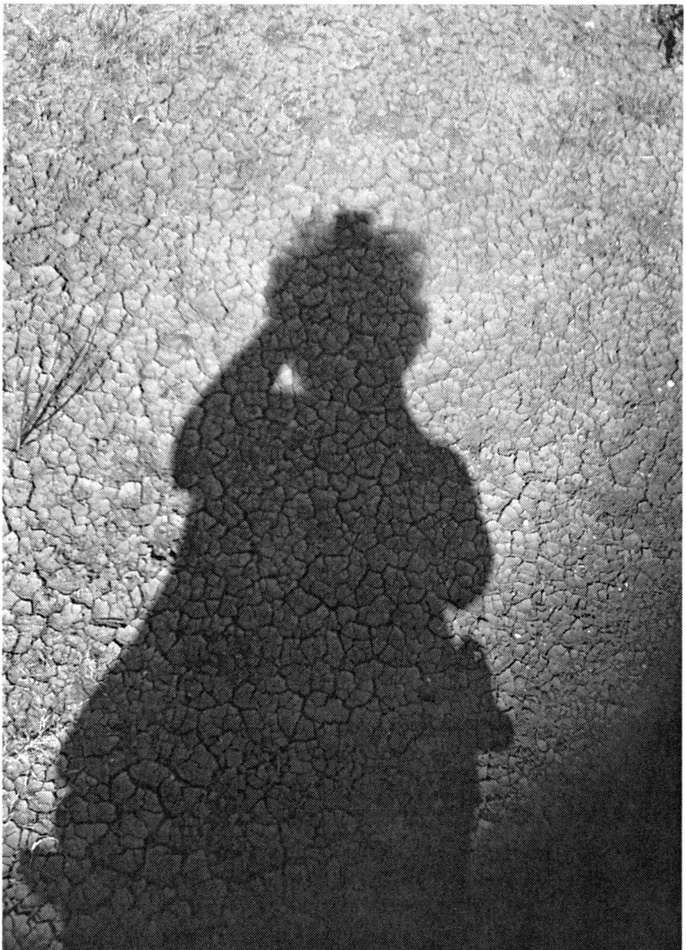

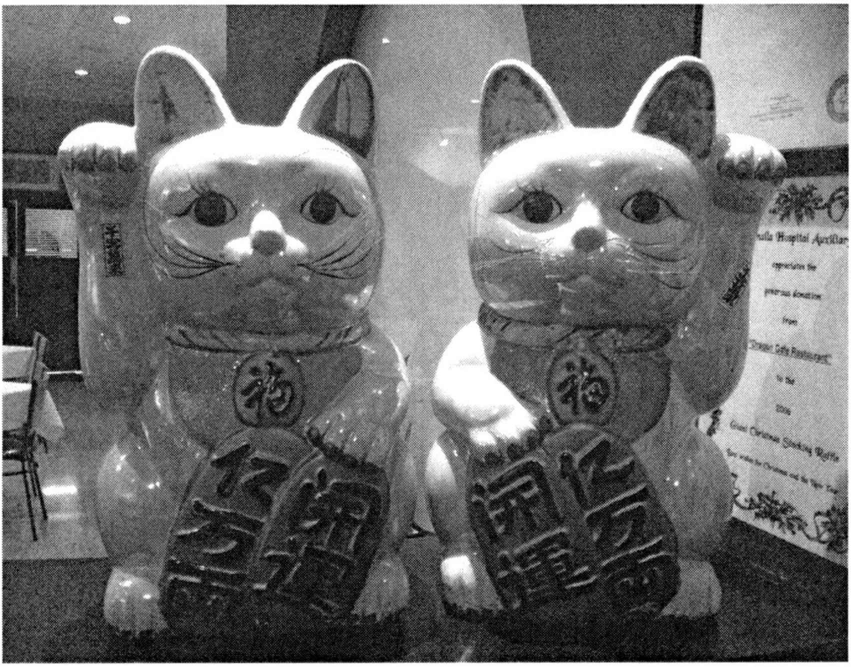
福
福

Waiting for rain

Talk is cheap
in this opportunity shop

('Just a drought,' the old men say)

as I touch the frosted rims
of 1950s tumblers,
run the spines of a row of
condensed books,
breathe in bridesmaid dresses
and lace curtains.

Next — Lake Cooper — bone dry.
A long list of birds on the board

waiting to return.

(A ghost
   wind
shifts in the reeds.)

— Like the mice,
rustling
in the hessian walls
of my brother's kitchen.

— And Spike,
with his Christmas bone
in April.

I step gingerly through
a shower of rose petals
that bloody the path
to the shed

where all that remains
is a set of false teeth
on a fruit box,

and lost in an untouched
bank-account,
a fist-full of wool money.

Outside, in the yellow grass
the sun rests down
on a rusting harvester.

('Just a drought.')

And the earth turns
from us / to us
as we dream.

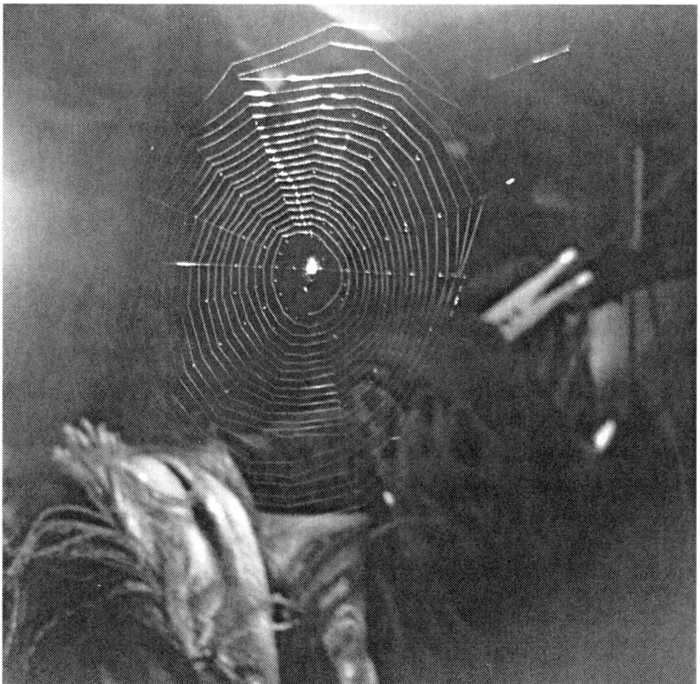

Singing us home

In a kitchen in Brisbane
three of us sit sharing tea
and talking about
dislocation
how hard we find it
to feel really *here*,
to feel we belong.

Each of us an
unplanned baby.
(An accident, or a surprise if you're being nice.)

Never felt that sense of
unequivocal right-to-be,
to take up space.

Margaret (from *Aotearoa*)
says that in Maori culture
a child is sung in,
called into being by her family.

We sit in silence
pondering this.

She pours more tea and
tells us about her grandmother
saying one day in exasperation
'You will never feel at home until you understand this —
Tūrangawaewae.

'My home is where I stand.'

A soft breeze enters and lifts the
hairs on my arms.

Suddenly the room
is filled with the most beautiful singing
like whale sounds

as Margaret sings us in.

We sit there
tears streaming down our faces
and come home.

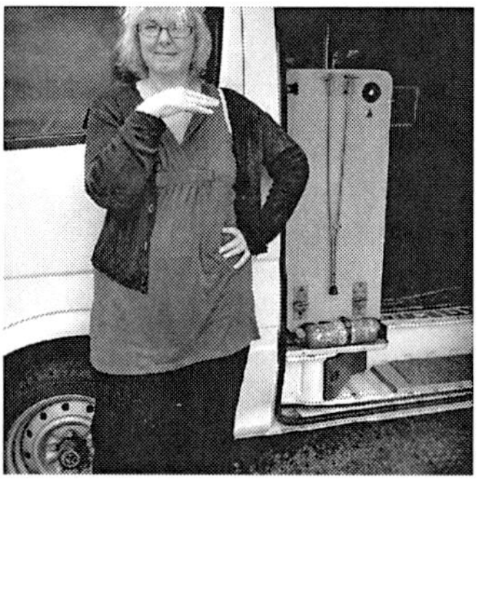
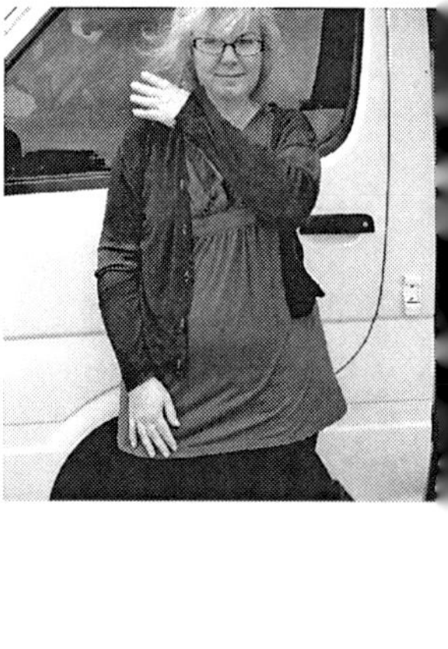

Notes on the text and acknowledgements

Some of these poems have previously been published in various versions in *Southerly, The Canberra Times, Overland, Westerly, Writing it Real,* and in the anthology *A Slow Combusting Hymn,* edited by Jean Kent and Kit Kelen (ASM/Flying Islands, 2014).

'The foot feels the foot when it feels the ground' is from Ernest Wood's 1971 *Zen Dictionary* (pp 91–2).

Erina Fair, for those not on the Central Coast, NSW, is the largest single-storey shopping complex in the Southern Hemisphere, and the largest Australian shopping complex outside of a metropolitan area.

My apologies to Dorothea Mackellar for mis-appropriation of some of the words from *My Country* and to Peter Dodds McCormick, likewise, for *Advance Australia Fair.*

'Declare War on 1024' (in 'Dreaming home') was an advertising campaign in the late 1960s aimed at reducing the Australian road toll, which the previous year was 1024 deaths from motor vehicle accidents.

My thanks to a range of anonymous bloggers for the tips and information used in 'Advice for van-dwelling', accessed online circa February 2009.

The historical information used in the found poem 'The road to recovery' is adapted from various tour guides and National Parks, Victoria websites and from an information board located on the Great Ocean Road. Recently a Portland man, Mr Iain Grant, has begun compiling a list of the names of those who helped build the Great Ocean Road. If you have information regarding this, he can be contacted at ij.grant@bigpond.com.au.

The Thomas Moore referred to in the subtitle of 'To the whales at Warnambool' is the author of *The Dark Night of the Soul* (NY: 2005).

'And now for a tincture of chaos' in 'Structure vs Blog' is a reference to the theme song of the 1960s cartoon series *Milton the Monster* ('And now for a tincture of tenderness…').

Thanks also to Anita Hoare for (among many things) her misquotation of a line from *The Flintstones*' theme song which I borrowed for 'The Party of Life'.

And a shout out to the country farmer-artists who created the Santa sculptures in various parts of Victoria for the delight of passers-by.

'Lost Woman Looks for Herself' is adapted from news reports, in particular a report dated 27th August 2012 from the *Iceland Review Online,* titled 'Lost Woman Looks for Herself in Iceland's Highlands'.

The Littlest Hobo (USA) and *Adventure Island* (Australia) are both children's television series from the 1960s. 'Maybe Tomorrow', the theme song of the *The Littlest Hobo* was written by Terry Bush. *Adventure Island* scripts and songs were written by John Michael Howson and the series was developed and produced by Godfrey Philipp.

My sincere thanks to Margaret Graham and Sue Wilkinson for that day in the kitchen in Brisbane that inspired the final poem 'Singing us home'.

Thanks also to Brendon Judkins for his comment used at the end of 'De-posession'; to Lynne Santos for her creative direction for the instead-of-a-suicide party; and to Claudia and Fairy for some great walks at the Lilyfield Dogpark.

The photographs used throughout are mine, with the following exceptions: the workers constructing the Great Ocean Road in the 1920s that faces the poem 'The Road to Recovery' (photographer unknown); the Twelve Apostles facing the start of 'The Shipwreck Coast', which was taken by my mother, Iris Spencer; and the strip of photos of me shoo-ing away flies on pages 146–7, which were taken by my sister-in-law Jean Spencer. Thanks to these photographers, and to Terri-ann for asking 'Would you consider adding photographs to the book?'

I owe enormous thanks to Ian Wansbrough for being there at the end of the phone for encouragement and superb editing advice – in particular during that amazing week in the final stages of writing – and for so many other times too. You helped make it possible and you helped make it fun.

Gratitude and love also to the following for being the first readers of *Vagabondage* and for cheering me along – Anita Hoare, Claudia Taranto, Helen Kundicevic, Kathleen Petersen, Sarah St Vincent Welch, Paul Brick and John Wright; and for feedback and courage, Catherine Moffat and Jennifer Kremmer.

Finally, thank you to my very patient agent, Jenny Darling; and huge thanks to Terri-ann White and all at UWA Publishing – I couldn't have wished for a better publisher.

This book is dedicated, with thanks, to all those who provided me with safe harbour in some form during my year in a Van, 2009–2010.

CPSIA information can be obtained
at www.ICGtesting.com
Printed in the USA
FSOW01n1335090914
3099FS

9 781742 586342